PRAISE FOR *INSPIRATION TO*

"Inside these pages is an abundance of wisdom from dynamic and brilliant women who have poured out the contents of their hearts and heads to provide a power packed tool for success."
— ROBIN FISHER ROFFER, AUTHOR, *MAKE A NAME FOR YOURSELF*

"NEW, the organization Christine Kloser founded, provides invaluable service and support to women who are looking to realize their professional and creative dreams. *Inspiration to Realization* encapsulates the best advice she and her members have to offer. Very inspiring!"
— SUSAN PIVER, AUTHOR, *THE HARD QUESTIONS*

"*Inspiration to Realization* is packed with wisdom and tools to help your dreams come true. If you're ready to create the life you've always desired, this book is for you!"
— TERRI AMOS, AUTHOR, *MESSAGE SENT: RETRIEVING THE GIFT OF LOVE,* AND FORMER MISS USA 1982

"I do want it all—and sometimes I feel completely overwhelmed. The women in *Inspiration to Realization* remind me to honor my spirit during my quest to achieve my dreams. Thank you, Christine, for bringing together women who are willing to share their struggles and successes. Their stories give me new ideas for creating the life I want and the courage to explore my options!"
— CATHERINE SEDA, INTERNET EXPERT AND AUTHOR, *SEARCH ENGINE ADVERTISING*

"*Inspiration to Realization* is wonderfully inspirational and ahead of the curve."
— MARCIA ISRAEL-CURLEY, AUTHOR, *DEFYING THE ODDS* AND FOUNDER, JUDY'S SPECIALTY STORES

"This book is filled with many gems to nurture your self-awakening and lifelong success in all that you create from the inside out. Treat yourself to this feast of wisdom from a unique gathering of Wise Women."
— CARISTA LUMINARE-ROSEN, PH.D., DIRECTOR OF EDUCATION, INNER SECURITIES, INC.

"Wow, what a great book! Each chapter is packed with valuable information to help all of us achieve greatness in our business and personal lives."
— ROBBIE MOTTER, OWNER CONTACTS UNLIMITED AND THE NAFE WESTERN & MID ATLANTIC REGIONAL COORDINATOR

"*Inspiration to Realization* is a must read for every woman pursuing her passion. It captures the essence of what women want to know about going from inspiration to realization of their dreams. Meet this amazing cast of women who share their wisdom and teach others how to go for the gold of life...happiness."
— MAUREEN O'CREAN, CO-AUTHOR *I AM DIVA, EVERY WOMAN'S GUIDE TO OUTRAGEOUS LIVING*

"Like listening in at quilting bee or an honest conversation between friends, *Inspiration to Realization* is a treasure chest of women's wisdom."
— MERYL MARSHALL-DANIELS, MEDIATOR, FACILITATOR AND CONSULTANT, FORMER PRESIDENT OF THE ACADEMY OF TELEVISION ARTS & SCIENCES

"Good for you. You've just picked up a very inspirational book that clearly shows how to create the life you've been dreaming of."
— KATHY AARONSON, AUTHOR, CEO, THE SALES ATHLETE, INC.

"The information and personal stories in *Inspiration to Realization* provide women everywhere with the tools and vision to go for their dreams."
— LINDA WESSELS, CEO, CONSULTCENTRAL

"How I would have treasured a book like this at the crossroads in my life. It is brimming with heartfelt warmth, tender truth and penetrating insights. Thank you to all the women of NEW, for sharing your deep wisdom with us."
— MOIRA SHEPARD, FOUNDER, REHAB DIVA

"*Inspiration to Realization* will teach and inspire you to focus on a purpose filled life of significance. You will enjoy and treasure the many life lessons."
— NICKI KEOHOHOU, CEO AND CO-FOUNDER OF THE DIRECT SELLING WOMEN'S ALLIANCE

"This recipe book for success isn't only for women. Guys, if you have any business relationships with women, Inspiration to Realization is a must read!"
— STU ZIMMERMAN, CEO OF INNER SECURITIES, INC., WWW.INNERSECURITIES.COM

"Wisdom says to learn from others. *Inspiration to Realization* takes you on the life dreams, journeys, lessons and blessings carved out of the lives of extraordinary women."
— ROBERT WHITE, PRESIDENT, ARC WORLDWIDE

"This is a magnificent book. It's clear, intentional and inspired! A book whose time has definitely come."
— AKUYOE GRAHAM, FOUNDER, SPIRIT AWAKENING FOUNDATION

"*Inspiration to Realization* is a must for every woman's library. From finances to food, this manual carves a road for women desiring to become wiser and healthier."
— JAN MARQUART, LCSW IS THE AUTHOR OF *ECHOES FROM THE WOMB*

"Now more than ever, women are called to stand up and lead... to inspire and remind all of humanity that life is truly sacred. You hold in your hands a book that demonstrates that true success is beautiful and we are absolutely the ones we have been waiting for! This book will give you multiple life orgasms. Read, apply, and enjoy!!!"

— Brigitte Secard, Creator of "The Joyfull Revolution" and
 Author of the hot new book, Soulfire: The Birth of Wild
 Aliveness

"Inspiration to Realization is like "Miso Soup for the 21st Century Woman's Soul." Now that women have been told for decades they can and should do everything (have careers, raise children and take care of a man), it is timely that women start helping each other to prioritize what is practical and appropriate for the uniqueness of each woman. Inspiration helps women celebrate their strengths and follow their hearts."

— Kartar Diamond, Author of Feng Shui For Skeptics: Real
 Solutions Without Superstition

"Before you struggle with your own mistakes, get the kernels of wisdom and keys to success from 41 brilliant women. Read this book and then begin your journey. If you've already begun, read it to make sure you're on the right road."

— Stewart Levine, Author, The Book of Agreement and Getting
 to Resolution

"As the book cover suggests, take that leap ladies! This book gives readers the inspiration along with the practical knowledge to be WOW—Women of Worth! Thanks for putting this incredible ride together!"

— Linda McCarthy, Executive Director of Business Network Int'l
 (BNI) of Ventura County

"After reading what the experts in this book have to say, you'll be inspired and activated to live the life you want!"

— Hyla Cass, MD, author of Natural Highs, and 8 Weeks to
 Vibrant Health

"These 41 women can definitely 'talk the talk' because they have 'walked the walk' on doing whatever it takes to empower themselves to ignite their level of success from within. They can help you, too, in creating a masterpiece each and everyday."
— VANESSA SUMMERS, AUTHOR, *GET IN THE GAME,* TELEVISION HOST, & MOTIVATIONAL SPEAKER

"How wonderful to have a comprehensive resource that supports the many facets of a woman's life. To be able to draw inspiration, reassurance and direction from these authors who have mastered their craft is an honor and a privilege."
— ELIZABETH REYNOLDS, EXECUTIVE ASSISTANT

"This book is filled with profound wisdom as it gently walks you through the process of creating a new, empowered reality."
— MARI SMITH, SUCCESS COACH, SPEAKER, TRAINER & AUTHOR

"As a mentor and coach, I work with women every day who clearly express some of the very same concerns that are addressed by the women in this book. While they grow their businesses and expand their wealth how do they get meaningful answers to their questions? What are the time-tested and proven strategies that will help them take action and expedite their goals? How do they find a clear direction that will help them win in the game of life? When readers open the pages of *Inspiration to Realization* they will find all of this and so much more."
— LORAL LANGEMEIR, *LIVE OUT LOUD* AND *WEALTH DIVA*

INSPIRATION
— TO —
REALIZATION

*This book is dedicated
to every woman
who has a dream in her heart
and the desire to turn
her inspiration into a realization.*

INSPIRATION

—— TO ——

REALIZATION

REAL WOMEN
REVEAL PROVEN
STRATEGIES FOR
PERSONAL, BUSINESS,
FINANCIAL AND
SPIRITUAL FULFILLMENT

COMPILED BY CHRISTINE KLOSER

Love
Your   Los Angeles, CA
Life

Published by Love Your Life

PO Box 661274, Los Angeles, CA 90066   USA

Published in the US and Canada by Love Your Life

ISBN 0-9664806-3-5

Library of Congress Control Number: 2004097825

www.InspirationToRealization.com
(310) 745-0794

SAN 256-1387

Book Design by Dotti Albertine

CONTENTS

Introduction

THANK YOU FOR PICKING UP THIS BOOK and reading it! One thing I probably know about you already is you're a woman with a dream in her heart, and you're willing to do whatever it takes to achieve it! It has been a great honor to bring together 41 voices of women just like you. They're all women who have a dream. They're here to share their insight, wisdom, stories and strategies to help you live a fulfilling life.

One thing you may notice that's different about this book is it covers a vast range of topics. The reason? I wanted it to reach women from a vast range of backgrounds, ages and varied interests. Just like the women in this book who all have their own experiences, we know every woman on the face of this earth has her own unique story. It is important to address all the areas of a woman's life—her personal, business, financial and spiritual life.

As women, it is essential for us to have a well-rounded life. If we focus on business and forget about our personal or family life, then our business success doesn't feel nearly as good. If we only focus on our spiritual life, but don't take responsibility for our financial life, then we'll never experience true freedom. This book is about having it all, and it's written by 41 women who want you to have every dream you desire.

How did these particular women come together on this project? They are all members of the Network for Empowering Women Entrepreneurs, also known as NEW, a professional association I founded in 2000. They all responded with a resounding "yes" when I started seeking contributing authors to this book. Each submitted a chapter idea and went through a special screening process before acceptance. Then our true journey began to bring together hearts, souls and minds to create a book we hope will touch your heart, resonate in your soul and expand your mind.

Again, thank you for reading and letting us know how your dreams have come true! Please share it with a friend, send a copy to your mother, daughter, sister or colleague. The world needs more women who turn their inspirations into realizations. Let your spirit shine and enjoy your journey.

To your success,

Christine Kloser
www.NEWentrepreneurs.com

PART I

PERSONAL FULFILLMENT

CHAPTER 1

Roadmap To Retirement

(It's Not About The Money!)

ANDREA BUTLER

Retirement can be your best friend, or your worst enemy.

GOT THAT IRA IN PLACE? Social Security and Pension estimates correct? Comfortable with your health insurance plan? That's great! Really great! Good for you!

By the way, while you were doing all that great planning did it ever occur to you the way you earned that good income for the past 30 or 40 years has so defined and shaped who you are, that retiring may make you feel a little like a fish out of water?

Retiring is not like going on a vacation. Why? You're never going back! You don't work there any more! All your "on the job" colleagues won't really be your friends. All the power you have gained over those years will be gone! All that daily prestige, etc., gone, gone and gone!

Scared you, didn't I? Sorry, but I needed to get your attention.

You're going to be entering the second half of your life. New everything. And I mean everything. For many women retirement is the best thing that ever happened to them. For many others. . . well. . . it's not so good. You've heard the stories—depression, illness and the like. You know how the body can react to big life changes! You have to prepare in every other area of your life, just as much as you prepared financially. There are positive ways to "transition" to make retirement the best part of your life.

Close your eyes and project yourself into your retirement. How old are you? What is your life like? What will you do today? What type of clothes are you wearing? What is the local scenery like? Are you happy?

YOUR PERSONAL "ROADMAP TO RETIREMENT"

Take control of your destination by setting the compass on your roadmap to retirement. Even though it may seem that retirement is way down the road, it isn't. The average *first age* of retirement in this country is 56. Many continue some work until they are about 65, and generally live to be close to 80. So, by the time a woman reaches the age of 40, she is already "middle aged". She already has lived about half of her life, but still has the second half to plan and live for.

The task at hand is how do you make the second half all you've dreamed it would be? People often think there will be plenty of time in the future to figure things out. If one works hard and long, everything will eventually fall into place. Right? Unfortunately, it doesn't unless we take charge ourselves.

Most people have absolutely no idea how they will spend their second half. You probably know some who just keep on working, even though they are financially secure, simply because they wouldn't know what to do with themselves.

Unfortunately, many are afraid to take that first step to even start thinking about their future years. 77 million baby boomers in denial! Gaining a sense of ownership, hope, excitement and belief in the future can eliminate this fear. In my workshops, I coach individuals, couples, groups and employees to help them define their purpose in life, and then set a plan of action to realize their retirement goals.

So, why not start now. Today! Think of this as "transition" planning. Here are some questions relating to the various areas of life. Do yourself a favor and answer them in order to get moving in the right direction. And guess what—it's fun!

PERSONAL ISSUES

What are my personal strengths? What am I really good at doing? What gives me the greatest sense of accomplishment and/or pleasure? If money were not an issue, how would I be spending my time during the week? On weekends? What part of the day do I enjoy most? Doing what?

FAMILY AND FRIENDS

Consider spouses (present and ex), significant others, extended families, parents, children and grandchildren. Will the kids still be living with me when I retire? Will my parents depend on me (financially and emotionally)? Will I have to be physically there for them or would occasional phone calls work? If I had a new circle of friends, what would they be like?

WORK AND MISSION

Can I turn the hobby (ies) I love into a moneymaking opportunity (ies)? Will I continue to work full time? What types of activities will fill my day while I make money?

FINANCIAL AND SECURITY

What opportunities do I have now to increase my retirement "fund"? When I retire, what expenses will be reduced or eliminated? Will I want to downsize my current home or apartment?

HEALTH AND FITNESS

What can I do right now to start improving my health and fitness? Is there an exercise I love to do? Walking or swimming perhaps? What about my eating habits? Is the food I eat nutritious?

SOCIAL AND COMMUNITY

Do I like being around others? Am I interested in being part of a community or volunteering my time to share my knowledge? How will I make new friends?

SPIRITUAL AND EMOTIONAL

How am I really feeling towards my retirement? Excited? Afraid? Would I welcome the chance to get "in touch" with nature (or some other spiritual connection I may have)? Is now a good time to meditate?

PERSONAL HAPPINESS AND DEVELOPMENT

Are there things I have always wanted to pursue and learn more about? Would I enjoy doing something totally new and different? Are there any classes I would be interested in taking now (perhaps through a church, school or online)?

Now, that wasn't so hard, was it? Let's go further—

VALUES

You can anticipate what's important to you today, may not be important to you when you're 60+. How might your values shift once you've retired? Understand what they may look like, and use this knowledge to help form your future reality.

LIFE BALANCE

How do you see your life balance ahead? If financial security, or family and friends are your priority now, how might things change for you in the future? Maybe health and fitness will rise to the top of the list!

PERSONAL MISSION

Thinking about your personal mission is a way to get focused on where you're going. Articulating your unique direction in life and the reason you exist, acts as an emotional touchstone for unleashing powerful feelings. It is the fuel for propelling you toward your vision of who you want to become, and how you want to spend your retirement.

GOAL SETTING

Having written goals is another important step to achieving those things in life that are top priority. Stating specific, measurable, attainable, realistic and timely (SMART) goals, and then breaking them into steps with timelines, and determining "who will do what by when", will give you the roadmap necessary to drive forward and realize your dreams in every area of your life. Begin listing your "Master List" of personal goals today! And, don't forget to include visualizations and affirmations. It's the first exciting step on your delicious journey to the satisfying retirement you deserve.

YOUR PERSONAL RETIREMENT PROJECTION

Now, just for fun, close your eyes once again and project yourself into your retirement. How old are you? What is your life like? What will you do today? What type of clothes are you wearing? What is the local scenery like? Are you happy? Aren't you glad that you took those extra few hours a week to plan this day?

Congratulate yourself for beginning your journey and determining your destination on your roadmap to "your perfect" retirement.

ANDREA has been designing and facilitating personal improvement programs for more than 25 years. Her most recent success is the "Roadmap to Retirement" workshop, where she helps people realize their retirement goals by careful planning in a comprehensive, upbeat workshop. Andrea was a pioneer in the "non-financial" aspect of retirement and is now considered an expert in the field. You can reach Andrea at: andrea@roadmaptoretirement.com www.roadmap-toretirement.com

CHAPTER 2

The Princess In The Tower Syndrome

JENTANA DABBS

I DISCOVERED IN MY OWN JOURNEY OF SELF-HEALING—a pattern, a metaphor. What was happening in my life and other women's lives was similar to the stereotypical fairytale princess trapped in a tower. In these fairytales, the princesses are generally characterized as weak, fragile victims, sometimes held captive in a tower. My big "aha!" was when I realized some women have unknowingly created an internal imprisonment made solely of negative thought. As we think more negative thoughts, another brick is formed, adding to the tower and building it even higher. This makes it more difficult to see the real truth about our world and us in it. This fairytale is a metaphor about how our own internal beliefs and consciousness influence our reality. For instance, if your thoughts and actions are negative, if you are self-absorbed, or are feeling victimized by a problem, you will remain "imprisoned." Sometimes, however, we must have darkness before we become willing to see the light.

THE TOWERS

Too often we focus on externals. Rather than looking within, we get too caught up in judgment and wanting. These judgments keep us trapped in our illusions and our old habit patterns, where we become a prisoner.

There is a land with many princesses, all very unique, talented, smart and beautiful in their own special ways. Unfortunately, all of these princesses are imprisoned in their own cold, dark, lonely tower created by dissatisfaction and uncertainty, and guarded by a ferocious, frightful dragon. There is only one way out. Every tower has a small window where a loving ray of sunlight from the outside shines in; this is our light that helps us to see the truth to set us free. Sadly, these princesses do not see the light.

By holding onto false ideas about ourselves, we limit our growth, which results in our frustration and constant pursuit of satisfaction and fulfillment outside of ourselves. Forgetful of who we really are and where we come from, we remain trapped in a prison of fear and uncertainty.

It is her own way of thinking that keeps a princess imprisoned in her tower, feeding the nasty dragon and manifesting yet another brick, making her tower grow higher, making it seemingly impossible to ever escape.

By affirming negative beliefs, we unknowingly use a power to create things we don't want to experience.

THE REFLECTION OF INNER SELF

What we are experiencing on the outside is a manifestation of our own inner thinking. It is our own beliefs that attract people who treat us this way and place us in situations.

Choosing to believe they were helpless victims of circumstance and that all was hopeless, the universe supported the princesses in this belief and kept them imprisoned, creating on the outside that which they created on the inside.

INTO THE DRAGON'S PIT OF FIRE

So dark is our tower, so dim is our light that we give others our power and lose all our fight. Prey we become for those who are weak to feed on our energy by lies they will speak.

This tale tells of various princesses who have found themselves tricked into the fiery pit of the dragon's dungeon. For example, Princess Catherine, who trusted a con-man prince who abused her mentally and physically, and then she escaped homeless and penniless. There was Princess Beth, who stayed with a cheating prince for two years, suffering much mental abuse; she stayed with him for fear of losing the lifestyle he provided her. Both princesses were looking for happiness and security outside them, only to attract that which they most feared most. They were treated externally the same way they treated themselves internally.

Through darkness of thought does darkness appear, in reality we summon that which we fear.

THE VICTIM MENTALITY AND SELF-PUNISHMENT

How foolish for us to punish ourselves in the present moment because someone hurt us in the past.
—Louise L. Hay

Alas, in sadness and despair, some of these wonderful princesses have punished themselves due to inflicted pain from others. We talk again of Princess Catherine, who, after escaping her abusing con-man prince, she puts herself in a dark dungeon to prostitution to strange men every day, all for money. *"I felt I had no choice! It was all I could do, and this was my only option!"* she said. And we

talk again of Princess Beth, who woke up in a hospital bed after trying to take her life with alcohol and sleeping pills, because she
could no longer take the pain.

THE POWER OF RELEASING AND SEEING TRUTH

*It often takes a crisis to break our usual models of the world; a cri-
sis is a gift, an opportunity, and perhaps a manifestation that life
loves us, by beckoning us to go beyond the dance we presently perform.*
—Leslie Lebeau

Through the darkness, however, the princess does find the
light to freedom; for once, the princess discovers and welcomes in
her own self love. She lets the light of love fill her imprisonment
and turns to face herself in the mirror affirming, *"Mirror, Mirror, I
see an image of someone as someone to be, here where I stand, show
me the someone, the true someone I am." "Oh god of the heavens
enough is enough; I open myself to shatter the patterns of life where
I have been stuck. I ask for vitality, I ask for empowerment to help me
to fight and break through the darkness moving into the light. To the
heavens I give trust to lead me from the darkness of this tower I ask
you at this moment that you allow me back my power. My spirit will
move now as a child of youth; I will open my eyes now for God to
show me the truth."*
At that moment, she opens her eyes to see her reflection in the
mirror; it has a beautiful white light around it as a message. *"The
truth is in our deepest being; we hold what is true inside of us. No one
can change the truth of who we are, for what we are made of is what
we believe we are. By finding your inner guide and love, which is hidden within you, and trusting it, for it is the very center of your being, it
will take you exactly where you need to go. Your inner guide will light
the way for you. Grasp onto this light for even the smallest amount will*

show you the door that sets you free. When you see the door, don't give it even a flicker of thought; just simply walk through it."

She then notices a little gold key has suddenly manifested itself around her neck, or had this key been there all along? She hurries out the door and down the steps. As she approaches the door to exit the tower, a huge terrifying dragon leaps between her and the door with its wings spread wide and large sharp teeth and fire shooting out of its nostrils. He looks down at the princess with an evil smirk on his face.

The princess stands her ground, as she looks up at him with a laugh, she says, "You have no more power over me." Just like that, she walks right through him, as if he was transparent, and steps out the door into freedom.

There is no power in the universe but ourselves that can free us from our own tower and stand up to our dragon.

JENTANA DABBS CCHT, NLP, is an expert Image and Life transformation Therapist who's Total Mastering System and cutting-edge techniques, such as Timeline Therapy and Cellular Release System, gently clear unwanted thinking patterns. She teaches mind-opening, transformational workshops to dynamically master the way toward the life you deserve. Jentana has a private practice in the West L.A. and Tarzana area and is available for speaking. www.totalmasteringsystems.com Jentana Dabbs can be reached at (866) 499-6545 EMAIL jentanad@yahoo.com

CHAPTER 3

The Man Plan

Finding & Catching Your Guy

JULIE FERMAN

SO. YOU WANT A MAN IN YOUR LIFE.

No sweat.

Really! Finding and catching your man is a simple, though not always easy process. Here's how to BE and what to DO, to develop the plan to reveal and deliver to you. . . your prince.

BE CLEAR—WHO *IS* THIS GUY?

It's brainstorm time. Make your long list of the qualities you're seeking in your mate. Go wild, have some fun with it. Then isolate the top three critical criteria. Tough? You bet, but so important. Keep this short list handy, wrestle with it and then revise it over time.

BE A MAN MAGNET

Men are drawn to warmth, spunk, wit, a loving spirit and an air of "come hither femininity." Men are visual creatures; they respond to color on the lips and cheeks, pretty skirts and shoes. Men love hair; don't chop it off. They love that hourglass shape; discipline yourself to exercise routinely and maintain a healthy diet. If you're venturing online to meet Mr. Right, post professional quality, current face and body photos. Craft your essays carefully to reveal your softer, nurturing side. Exercise and play on your femininity in person. Use your girly nature to catch his eye and win his heart.

BE A KEEPER COLLECTOR

Hello101. Saying hello to that nice looking gent at the car wash is for some natural, and for others. . . a learned skill, which you are now going to develop. YOU are going to begin the practice of chatting up total strangers in line at the supermarket, the deli, and the dry cleaners—in fact, just about everywhere you go. Practice first on sweet old ladies, moms with kids, and then. . . the men. Hit the mute button on that cowardly little voice in your mind as it reliably offers discouraging, deflating, self-critical negativism. Rather, focus outward, on brightening the day of each person who crosses your path. Offer a sincere compliment, ask if the Lean Cuisine he's purchasing is any tastier than the one in your freezer. Ask him if he likes his car, or heck, what time it is—the topic isn't important, but the social magnetism you're developing is.

The introduction. In the midst of this casual conversation, slip in "Oh, I'm Julie, by the way. What's your name?" Offer your hand to shake or reach out with a warm touch to the shoulder, instantly transforming this 'stranger' into a new 'contact'. Weave into the chat a reference to your work or your social life, and run with him down any conversation avenue he offers. Mention the fun gatherings, which you and your single friends attend and host, inquire about where he lives or works, and ask the simple but powerful question, "Just curious, are you a single person or a happily attached person?" Be fully present, open, and welcoming, remembering that your other-focused eye contact and warm smile is a gift to him and to everyone you touch throughout the day.

Take him home. Well, sort of. . . Try out these closers: "I'm so glad we met. You're a keeper. Let's stay in touch. Here's how to reach me. My friends and I are always planning fun social gatherings; shall I invite you? Share your email address or phone number with me and we'll include you." Have business or personal cards printed up and always easily accessible in your purse or pocket, and a pen too, to jot down his contact info if he doesn't offer his card.

Hook your fishy. When you get home, within 24 hours of meeting, shoot off a warm, inviting email or place a quick, cheerful call, saying how nice it was to bump into him. Suggest chatting again over coffee. See if a dialogue begins.

These "chance encounters" are in my terms, critical opportunities for relationship. With each casual hello, you are becoming more sticky, more comfortable and proficient with the process of initiating and developing new contacts, connections, friends and prospective partners. Collect your keepers, develop your 'little black book' and before you know it, you'll have enough new friends to throw that party you've been talking about. . . !

DO THE PICKY TEST

My biggest frustration is watching GREAT people overlook and dismiss other GREAT people for superficial reasons. Take the "Am I being too picky?" test now. Consider closely the last 10 to 20 candidates who've crossed your path. Study the men you've dated, selected through an online service, met through business or friends—candidates you deemed interesting and attractive. Keep this list and continue adding to it into the future for objective statistical analysis.

Note by each name if he was also interested in YOU. Was he attracted to you? Did he pursue you? If less than 25% on your hit list are also going for you, then I say you're being too picky, limiting yourself too much to expect success.

WHAT TO DO IF YOU FLUNKED THE PICKY TEST?

1. Re-evaluate and open up your standards. Stretch on the issues of lesser importance (height, hair preferences, age, income, living location). If a new candidate meets your top three critical criteria, engage him and meet him, even if he doesn't WOW you upon first glance.
2. Broaden your reach, play the numbers game, do some serious strategic marketing to better your chances in our highly competitive romantic culture. Join dating services and singles clubs and be proactive while there, develop your flirting skills, meet lots and lots of men.

Whereas men are typically visual and need to be physically attracted from the start, we women can develop attraction and fall in love over time. Keep the heart and the eyes open, and be willing to be surprised as to who He just might turn out to be.

If the guy you're considering has all of your Top Three Critical Criteria, I suggest (and so would your mama) err on the side of WhatTheHeckMeetTheGuy. A wise grandmother once advised me, "Julie, never turn down a date with anyone. . . you never know who his friends might be!" That southern belle had men chasing her well into her seventies.

DO YOUR ACTION PLAN

If your personal goal is be in a loving partnership within the next year of your life, then I want you on an average of two first dates each month with new prospective candidates—men who meet your top three critical criteria and who are also interested in you. What vehicles should you use to meet and hook these fishies? Singles events, business mixers, online dating sites, register privately with me, gather your friends and throw parties, flirt and schmooze everywhere you go, and actively reach out to the men who interest you.

Do whatever it takes to get on those two new dates each month. Not sure after the first date? See him again. Still not sure? See him one more time, as research shows—the much sought after and heartwarming magic called human bonding doesn't even begin until date number three.

BE YOUR BEST YOU

Get in shape and stay in shape, inside and out, keep learning and growing, reading and taking classes. Doing so keeps you fresh and alive. Constantly explore and develop the inner you, balance your inner work with a GetOutThere plan, including registering privately with me at www.CupidsCoach.com. Extend invitations, be available and accessible, focus outward, offer your willing smile, your engaging eyes, and use a warm, sweet greeting on your voice mail. . . you'll be getting lots of calls. . .

JULIE FERMAN is Cupid's Coach. She founded her web-based matchmaking service to dignify and simplify the love search process for desirable, selective, relationship-minded professionals. A product of the dating service industry (her 13 year marriage was the result of a Man Plan of her own) and with over 1,000 marriages to her credit. . . she's here to help you. Singles of all ages are invited to register with Julie privately, for free, at www.CupidsCoach.com Visit the Events and Service tabs or call 877-345-LOVE

CHAPTER 4

How To Take Care Of Yourself First

JJ FLIZANES

YOU WORK 14-HOUR DAYS, SIX DAYS A WEEK. Your day off is the day you set aside to run errands to keep the other six days going. The kids need to be cared for; you need to run the business, and your spouse hasn't seen you relaxed in years. Does this sound like you?

We try to do it all and expect that somehow, magically, we will survive while moving at 150 miles per minute. Surveys have shown two-thirds of the American population has sleeping problems; they can't get a restful sleep, or they don't sleep enough. Two out of six Americans are obese, and heart disease is the number one cause of death in the United States. But this is ALL preventable. So why do we make the choice to ignore our own health? Why don't we utilize the principles we apply to other things like our family, our cars and our homes?

Several years ago, I started my parents on a training program. I had been home for the holidays and trained them each individually. I made their own "specialized" plan as to what they were to do, as I taught them how to do it.

After I left, I checked back to see if they were working out on their own. Of course their answer was "no." After several weeks of hearing "no," I decided to make a video on my next trip home. I said, "Do you miss me? Well, watch the tape and work out!"

After my brother and I filmed this 30-minute workout, I gave them one month to do the tape three times. I threatened if they did not exercise three times in the month, I would hire a trainer to come to their home. Now, you may be asking yourself, why did I threaten them? Are they overweight? No. Are they unhealthy with heart disease or high cholesterol? No. They are healthy, and I want them to stay that way!

As we age, we lose hormones. Losing hormones means we lose muscle mass at a faster rate if we are not building muscle. Losing muscle means losing strength and bone density; our metabolism decreases, and we have an increased risk of injury and gaining weight if we continue to eat the way we did prior to this "age" change.

The good news is that it is all preventable! You can preserve and build bone, build muscle and increase your metabolism, gain strength and energy and be as strong or even stronger than ever! The challenge is that you have to make a commitment to take care of YOU, and it will require time and effort.

It is your choice, and I am here to help you make the healthier choice so you will not only look and feel your best, but you will be better able to help those you love live longer and work more efficiently.

Did you know you can make more money and work better when you exercise?

Exercise causes the brain to release endorphins, which are opium-like substances that ease pain and produce a sense of comfort and euphoria. It also encourages the nerve cells in the brain to secrete other neurotransmitters such as serotonin, dopamine and norepinephrine, which improve general feeling. Deficiencies of these hormones and enzymes have been linked to symptoms of depression, anxiety, impulsivity, aggression and increased appetite.

According to the results of a new study reported in the American Medical Association's Archives of Internal Medicine, researchers found when depressed patients exercise, they are actually able to increase the levels of these natural antidepressants. We now know there is sound research that links exercise and its positive effect on our emotions and therefore our behavior. Now how do you get started?

First, I would suggest doing a time management exercise of counting how many hours per week you spend on different tasks. We all have seven days, which equals 168 hours per week. How do you spend your time?

I divided mine into seven categories.

Office Time:	11 hours
Client time:	19 hours
Class time:	4 hours
Networking:	35 hours
Travel Time:	50 hours
Workout time:	4 hours
Sleeping:	45 hours

Once you begin to see where you spend your time, you can see where you can exchange time that isn't spent productively. Obviously I saw that I spend most of my time in my car traveling between appointments, class and networking. If I wanted to spend more time reading or working out, I could rearrange my schedule to get some of my driving time down.

Next, you need to clarify your goals. Are you happy with your current state of health? Are you happy with your body? If you could take a magic wand and change some things about your fitness and health, what would they be? Write them down.

Try on some clothes that you don't think will fit. I like to tell clients to try on the skirt or pair of pants that are a little snug or used to fit and then look in the mirror.

Rather than saying negative things to yourself, congratulate yourself for taking action. Get excited about how your body will change when you start taking care of it. This is the exciting part! You can change it! Now put the items in the back of your closet and leave them there for eight weeks.

At this point, I suggest taking measurements and perhaps consult with an educated and experienced trainer to record some girth measurements and body fat—you can use the scale too, but keep in mind the scale should *not* be used more than once a week. Numbers are a way to gauge progress.

If you were to weigh yourself on three different scales, you might have three different readings. Numbers can also be abused so be careful not to give too much importance to them. Doing a low-carbohydrate, high protein diet (which I *strongly* recommend *against*), will make your body lose water weight quickly.

If you stepped on the scale and saw the quick loss, you might get excited. But these results are fleeting. If you decided to have a muffin or piece of bread, and the next day stepped on the scale to see you had now gained two pounds—you might be very upset.

Evaluate your emotional attachment to all of this and do what you think is best for you. If using the scale will make you crazy—then don't use it. Have a trainer take some measurements, throw out the scale, and use the clothing example instead.

Now it's time to make a plan. If it's in the budget, I would suggest working with a highly educated and qualified trainer. Having someone else to support and guide you will probably make all the difference in the world. If this is not an option, call a friend or relative who would like to take better care of him/herself as well and actually schedule time to exercise—you must make yourself accountable! Keep a daily log of what you eat so you can review it.

Assess what is working and how to make it better; then give yourself small rewards along the way for a job well done—you deserve it!

⌐⟋⟍

J.J. FLIZANES is the director and founder behind Invisible Fitness. She was selected as one of the top six personal trainers for 2003 by Shape Magazine and is a spokesperson for the American Heart Association. J.J. has been featured on NBC, KTLA CBS and has appeared in many national magazines such as Fitness, Muscle and Fitness HERS, Elegant Bride, E Pregnancy, and more. Invisible Fitness can be reached at (800) 571-5722 and at www.invisiblefitness.com

CHAPTER 5

How To Be Your Own Best Matchmaker

Four key ingredients for "cooking" up the relationship you're craving

JULIE HAYES

AS THE OWNER OF A SUCCESSFUL DATING AGENCY and having gone through the dating "mine field" myself for the past "umpteen" years, I have learned a thing or two about what it takes to be a good matchmaker. However, no matter how good anyone is at being a matchmaker for other people, the ultimate decision lies with the one who is being matched up, and in your case this is YOU! I'd like to share four key ingredients so you can go out into the world and learn "How To Be Your Own Best Matchmaker."

I'm going to list ideas, many of which you've heard before, but you might need to be reminded of before you actually put them into practice. Whether you're currently single and looking to find that special someone, you're in a relationship in which neither party is completely happy, or you're going through a bad break-up or loss of some kind, these four ideas will get you back on track with the love life you're intended to have.

Let's begin with the first one: *acceptance*. This means no matter what situation you're currently in, and no matter how sad or depressing you think it might be, you need to accept the circumstances and know you have the power to change them.

The second idea works hand-in-hand with acceptance, and it is *choice*. After you have truly accepted your current situation, you then need to make a choice to be happy about it. Now, you're probably saying to yourself, how can I choose to be happy if I really want to be in a relationship, and I'm still currently single. . . ? Or some other question to that effect. . . And here's my answer: You have to choose to be happy no matter what the circumstances are, because this choice alone will keep you at a higher vibration and will more easily allow the universe to start sending great things your way.

If you concentrate on the negative and spend the majority of your time thinking about how upset or angry you are about being single after all these years, or how angry you are at something your current partner did, then you keep yourself at a much lower vibration; and unfortunately by doing this, you will continue to attract more negative energy. However, if you choose to be happy even in your current situation, you keep yourself at a higher vibration and will naturally attract more positive energy towards you. This in turn, will allow your ultimate partner to automatically be drawn to you like a magnet.

I know from my own experience, any time a relationship ended, I was always able to move through the pain and sadness much sooner and more easily by focusing on positive things rather than wallowing in depression. For example, one time not so long ago, I felt sure I had found my soulmate. This wonderful man, whom I will refer to as "D," had all of the values I had ever wanted in a man, and he was physically the type of man I had always dreamed I would marry. However, the "too good to be true" syndrome got to me; I started worrying about losing him "this marvelous treasure the universe had brought to me." Instead of focusing on the positive and truly enjoying just being with him in the present, I started focusing on the negative: my insecurities and the "what-ifs," (What if I lose him? What if I screw this up? Etc.) Ultimately I caused the demise of this relationship purely because of my negative thinking.

Now imagine if you will, the depression I wanted to feel about finally having found "the one" and then having thrown it all away just from negative thinking. However, instead of going down this path, I took my own advice and combined the first and second ideas with a third. I determined the universe would either provide me with another soulmate, who was more appropriate for me, or the universe would bring "D" and I back together for a second chance.

The third idea is remembering to be *in the present moment.* Not living in the present is what caused my relationship with "D" to fail. Everything was going so well, if only I had just focused on being and enjoying the present moment with him, we probably never would have broken up. Here's the lesson I want you to learn from my mistake: always, always appreciate what you have and enjoy it; really enjoy it in the moment! If more of us did this, I truly believe more couples would stay together because their focus would be on enjoying each other in the present moment and not focused on aggressions or upset from the past and insecurities or worries about the future.

If you're currently single and you live, act and think from the state of already being where you want to go as far as a relationship is concerned, then that state of being will show up much sooner. If you want to be in love, but have not currently found a partner to be in love with; you can still be in love, just be in love with yourself. I don't mean in an egotistical way, but know what you bring to the table, and as long as you are a good person, then you deserve the partner you've been craving. You will get him/her if you exude this confidence and positivity. Please remember idea #3, the state of being in and enjoying the present moment; it is extremely important.

The fourth and final idea, is *saying positive affirmations daily*. As previously mentioned, remaining positive and choosing to be happy will keep you at a higher vibration and will cause more positivity to be drawn to you.

After my relationship with "D" went south, instead of remaining in a depressed and powerless state, I chose to focus on the positive things in my life. I chose to be thankful that I had my health, my family, my home, my friends, my career and so on. What happened as a result is truly amazing. I kept myself at a higher vibration daily by concentrating on all those positive things, and almost instantly, more and more choices started to present themselves.

All of a sudden, I had many options to choose from for a lifetime mate, including a second chance with "D" if I wanted it. So you see, concocting your own relationship recipe really does work if you *accept* your current situation, *choose* to be happy by *being in the present moment*, and truly acting from a *positive* place of already being what it is you are craving. I once heard it is not the destination that is important, it is the journey, and who we are along the way that is. Along your journey of becoming your own best matchmaker, there will be some relationships that come to an end, but always remember, "Never look at anything from your past as a failure; there is no failure, there is only what's next!!"

JULIE HAYES was born in Cincinnati, Ohio and moved to Los Angeles immediately following college graduation. After running countless marketing campaigns for clients such as Procter & Gamble, Cadillac and The History Channel; Julie decided it was time for her own gig. She started a social event dating agency, Social Network Company, www.SocialNetworkCompany.com, which has been featured on Channel 7 KABC NEWS and the Fine Living Network. Julie is a seminar leader and keynote speaker.

CHAPTER 6

Your Thoughts. . .
Your Power

MARYLOU KENWORTHY

HOW EXCITING WOULD IT BE to learn you hold a powerful secret within you that could change your life quickly, easily and dramatically? All you would have to do is become aware of this secret and use it properly to create your dreams and desires. Yes, a whole new life is as close as. . . your next thought. Your thoughts are so very powerful that they truly do create your reality. Everything in life is created twice, first in your mind and then in your outer world.

THOUGHTS LEAD TO BELIEFS, LEAD TO FEELINGS, LEAD TO ACTION.

Have you ever kept trying and trying to accomplish something only to encounter obstacles? You may have thought something external was to blame when in fact it was an internal block. Perhaps you didn't *feel* confident about yourself and didn't *believe* you would succeed because nagging, negative *thoughts* kept spinning around in your head. No matter how much will power and drive you have, your internal (or subconscious) thoughts are driving your behavior and may be sabotaging your efforts. So, always start at the beginning—with thought.

Whether you think you're a loser or think you are a winner, you're right.
—Henry Ford

Are you aware of the thoughts that go through your mind during the day? What were you thinking as you rolled out of bed this morning, as you dressed, drove in traffic, waited in line, spilled your coffee? Are your thoughts supportive or toxic? Do you beat yourself up?

Another way to become aware of your thoughts is to pay attention to the words you use. Do you ever go out to lunch with "the girls" and jokingly put yourself down? Every time you say something like "Oh I was so stupid to . . ." you are telling your subconscious mind that you are stupid! Even if you were just kidding around, that negative label is added to the many other negatives in your programming (subconscious mind). That's another little secret—your subconscious mind doesn't have a sense of humor!

Are you a "yeah, but" person—always finding an excuse, a way out, or immediately blocking a new idea or way of doing things? Do you use weak or empowering words?

Weak Words	Empowering Words
I'm supposed to	I choose to
I should	I decided to
I need to	I want to
It's too hard or difficult	It's a challenge

STOP AWFULIZING!

What you focus on follows. Do you talk about your successes and the positive things in your life or do you complain, place blame, and express doubt and fear throughout the day? My favorite word (and you won't find it in the dictionary) is "awfulize". Don't you just love it? Some examples of "awfulizing" are: "I know I'm going to get the flu", "It's going to be another boring meeting", "I'll probably not get the job, not have fun on my date, not win the game, or not get the promotion". Since your thoughts create your reality, this negative chatter sets you up to experience exactly what you are complaining about.

EVERY THOUGHT WE HAVE AFFECTS US MENTALLY, EMOTIONALLY, PHYSICALLY, AND SPIRITUALLY.

Imagine you're having a lousy day, your energy is low, nothing is going right, and you feel like you want to go back to bed. Then let's say you receive a phone call from someone special in your life. You share some "good time" stories, love and laughter. How do you feel after the phone call? The day suddenly looks brighter, doesn't it? You feel emotionally and spiritually uplifted and are filled with renewed energy. What happened? Your thoughts changed, nothing more. How easy and magical is that?

HEY, THESE ARE SOMEONE ELSE'S BELIEFS!

Did you know that some thoughts and beliefs deep in your subconscious mind might be someone else's? Think back. . . was there ever a classmate, friend, sibling, teacher, coach, parent, or boss who put you down? Did anyone important to you ever say you weren't pretty, strong, popular, smart enough, or good enough? Could these negative beliefs be influencing you right now? Yes, many messages you received, especially as a child, still color who you are today.

While growing up, I adopted many beliefs from others that affected me deeply—"You're stupid and ugly", "No one wants to play with you", "What you have to say isn't important", "Girls can't be architects", and "Good little girls keep quiet". Do any of these messages sound familiar?

The rejection and putdowns I experienced while growing up instilled feelings of fear, lack and unworthiness and left me with low self-esteem and no confidence. I carried these thoughts, beliefs, and feelings into my adult life where they manifested in my outer experiences. Someone else's beliefs were running my life! I released this old "programming" through meditation, journaling, affirmations, hypnosis and imagery and took back control of my life. These techniques healed me, gave me the strength to leave a dangerous relationship, and the confidence to follow my dream. I am now living a free and fulfilling life empowering other women. You too can create a whole new reality for yourself.

CHANGE YOUR MIND AND YOU CHANGE YOUR LIFE.

There are four steps to using your powerful thoughts to change your life.
1. Awareness
2. Release
3. Replace
4. Reinforce

AWARENESS:
As you go through your day, notice what you're thinking and saying. Jot down thoughts that keep popping up and any phrases you repeat about yourself. Take a good look at them. Where did they come from (a teacher, parent, brother)? Are they beneficial to

you? What feelings do they bring up? Do this for a few weeks until you become so aware that you stop yourself and choose a more empowering thought or phrase.

RELEASE:

Pick the thoughts that do not serve you and write them down with the intention of releasing them. Look them over and vow to never say or think them again. Now, burn this list!

REPLACE:

Write down what you choose to think (and say) instead. Put these new words and thoughts on colorful cards if you'd like. Now, this is my favorite technique—Affirmations. These are statements that support you and your desires. I recommend a special way of doing affirmations that will get you quicker results—write them down before going to bed.

Affirmations are: Positive, Precise statements said (written) in the Present tense.

Examples:
- "I am worthy of . . ."
- "I choose to be happy and calm"
- "I am an excellent salesperson (speaker, mother, money manager . . .)"
- "I allow only good to flow into my life"
- "I am healthy and feel energized"

REINFORCE:

Visualizing your successes. Now that you are using new, supportive thoughts and words and your subconscious mind is growing comfortable with them, it's time to give these new thoughts more energy. Take a few moments at the end of the day, close your eyes and visualize yourself as that healthy, energetic mother, successful salesperson, worthy and beautiful woman, or money magnet—whatever you desire to manifest. Paint a picture for yourself. Make it as real as you can by using all of your senses. See, feel, hear, smell, and taste your success!

Become aware of your thoughts, release the toxic ones, create new thoughts that support you, and then bring them to life with your imagination. That's how to manifest your desires. You hold this secret power within you. Why not start using your thoughts to create the life of your dreams?

MARYLOU KENWORTHY, C.Ht., EFT-CC is an inspiring speaker, workshop facilitator, certified hypnotherapist and Emotional Freedom Technique (EFT) practitioner. MaryLou is the creator of Wings, a life-changing Empowerment Program for women, "Release" journals, and "Unique U" audio program, and author of "Stepping from Stress into Strength". Visit http://www.ThoughtMatters.net and sign up for Thought Matters Free monthly newsletter featuring tips and techniques designed to help you create a balanced, healthy, and fulfilling life. Contact: MaryLou@ThoughtMatters.net 818 203-2257.

CHAPTER 7

Outsmarting Overwhelm

SHAWN MOORE

YOU KNOW THE FEELING. It might be your brain racing with thoughts you can't quite decipher. Maybe it is a sudden sense of panic, like deer spotted in the headlights. We've all experienced it in one form or another—the feeling of being overwhelmed.

Overwhelm is an uncomfortable sense that everything is out of control and just beyond your reach. If you have ever witnessed your belongings being loaded onto a moving van, you know what I am talking about. It's a mix of emotional thoughts and feelings stirred up by events beyond your control. It's as though you wish you could fold your arms, (remember Jeannie from "I Dream Of Jeannie") and blink your eyes and have everything easily and beautifully placed in the perfect new location.

Like it or not, whatever our individual situation, most of us will encounter overwhelm at one time or another. It's just a fact of life.

By preparing ourselves to manage it, we will outsmart overwhelm. In the past few years, I have heard many prominent people describe how they found themselves in a total state of overwhelm just prior to experiencing big success. Please notice two important points: 1) successful people experience overwhelm, and 2) success still happens in their lives. Successful people don't let it stop them.

As I carefully listened to their victorious stories, I noticed something distinctly different in their choice of vocabulary than most people who struggle with overwhelm. Interestingly enough, they refer to overwhelm as a challenge and see it as something exciting to overcome; it requires their best skills to keep moving along their path to success.

But what if you are someone who does not think it is exciting? In fact you dislike being overwhelmed. What about those of us who feel like deer in the headlights? What can we do when the struggle takes pleasure out of our business? If you've lived on this earth for more than a few decades, you've had a chance to discover whether or not you're prone to overwhelm and how you handle it. Is it time to shift to a better tactic?

The choice is up to you. Will you let overwhelm get the best of you or will you overcome it and be the winner?

Your first action will be to make a plan. Plan to balance challenging times with some pleasant times. Schedule breaks, even if you are physically not able to leave the office. A short break will give you a fresh perspective, and it will allow your brain to rest. Author Stephen Covey refers to it as "sharpening the saw." Remember, the process of overwhelm has its highs and lows. It has stages and will transition from one to another before you know it, if you don't seek help.

WAYS TO COMBAT OVERWHELM BEFORE IT BRINGS YOU DOWN INCLUDE:

- Pack a 'care package' filled with healthy snacks to energize your body and mind if you have a work project that requires long hours.

- Chunk down the tasks. Set up your schedule and include a few minutes for breaks. Be realistic about the difference between a task and a project.
- Place fresh flowers on your desk. Just glancing at the flowers relaxes your eyes and relieves the stress of staring at a flat computer screen all day.
- Plan something to look forward to as a reward. Reinforce the plans, circle the date on your calendar; have pictures or symbols of the reward available for frequent viewing. Work toward the reward.
- Watch your language. Sometimes a situation is awful, but we can avoid the drama. How's your inner talk? Are you treating yourself in a way that you would not accept from others? Demeaning words to yourself will add frustration, fear and overwhelm.
- If it's possible for you to affirm the situation in a positive way, then do this repeatedly during the day. Even if you have to say it silently to yourself, do it! Please trust me on this, it will help you. If you can't think of a positive thing to say, then use a traditional affirmation such as "This too shall pass".
- Eat well. Healthy food supports your energy and prevents sluggishness. Eat good food to think clearly and maintain stable blood sugar levels for your emotions and stamina to be healthiest.
- Get as much sleep as you need and make it a priority when you are handling a demanding schedule. Remember the adage of "sharpening the saw"?
- Practice relaxation techniques, stretching, breathing, meditation and visualization throughout the day. These are great ways to break the cycle of work stress and help disengage after a busy day.
- Inject laughter to inject energy. Choose to laugh, get a joke book or a humorous daily calendar.

- Remind yourself of other times in your life when you lived through challenging times. You did it then; you will do it again.
- Ask for help when it is appropriate. You don't always have to do everything alone. Is it possible to ask a friend for help? Is this a situation where you can hire a professional consultant?
- Get advice from others who have gone through this same situation in their own life. Their story may give you guidance and much needed hope.
- Celebrate each phase of the process. Be honest and follow through with respect and care for yourself, your time and your energy.
- Use good supplies and tools when working on projects. With inadequate tools, we end up battling little aggravations that escalate and add to the sense of overwhelm.
- Do your work somewhere else. Shake things up and free yourself by altering your workspace. Sometimes our very habits will lead us into the pattern and routine of stress. By making a change, it might interrupt a negative pattern.
- Get perspective. Typically we aren't operating on overload or overwhelm in all areas of life. Thank goodness! This is a good time to consider all that you are grateful for. Take a look at your photo album and remind yourself you have a good life and meaningful relationships.
- Ask for help. Build a team. Do you have to learn to do the task or is your time better spent finding a specialist to perform it? For example, must you design your own website from scratch? Why not hire a great web designer?
- Follow the leaders. Think about how Eleanor Roosevelt, Oprah Winfrey, Mother Teresa, Abraham Lincoln, Albert Einstein, your favorite teacher or any person you have admired would advise you in your situation.

- Choose your battles. Take a closer look at your reactions. What would happen if you change your response to the situation? Could you alter your response and actually end up lowering your stress? Is it a mountain or a large molehill?
- Celebrate along the way. The thrill of taking on a new project is great, but unrealistic expectations can cause the sensation of overwhelm. Celebrating progress made helps you to gain momentum and provides a new wave of energy.
- Be aware of saboteurs. Guard yourself from negative people and their negative talk. Call a positive friend to get an attitude adjustment when needed.
- Could you be using a better system? Your state of overwhelm might be self-induced because of your organizational style. Maybe this is a good time to consult with a professional organizer to help you get on the right track.

One of the most important things you must have is an intense vision of "Your Why," the passion or purpose that drives you to work with a commitment to succeed. For some people, the "Why" is a reward or accomplishment that has nothing to do with the work at hand. It may be a deeply held personal dream they are going to fund with the money earned from their current hard work. Or it could be the immediate reward of personal satisfaction of a job well done. The vision of dream vacations, new homes and exceptional experiences shared with family or friends might be the reason why a person will endure the challenge of overwhelm with energy and grace.

You will have more energy and enthusiasm towards the project, the more passionate and clear you are about defining your "Why". Have pictures or mementos to keep your "Why" present and mindful while you go through the paces of manifesting it.

"If your why is big enough, you will find the way".

Take the steps to outsmart overwhelm and join the successful who passionately proclaim their "Why" all the way to the top.

⌒

Information gathering and sharing is SHAWN'S passion. Experienced working with community education projects, fundraising and advocacy programs she helped change lives and circumstances of clients served. Today she focuses on providing helpful tips and information about personal and professional development resources for entrepreneurs. Baroness Builders is a source that helps people find resources, hope, guidance and a fresh direction for their lives. She can be reached direct at 530.899.8299 or visit online at www.baroness-builders.com.

CHAPTER 8

Learn To Receive
As Much As You Give

VICTORIA KINDLE HODSON & MARIAEMMA WILLIS

I need more time!
I need more money!
I need more balance in my life!

THESE ARE THE THREE MOST COMMON needs expressed by our female colleagues, friends and clients as they strive to take the next step in their careers, maintain an active home life and somehow sneak in some time for themselves. There is a lot of giving to others going on in their busy lives, and they often feel exhausted and overwhelmed because they don't know how to balance the scales and get as much as they *give*.

Fifteen years ago, we started teaching parents and teachers how to meet the learning needs of children, but we quickly realized many of the adults we were talking to didn't know how to meet their own needs. Actually, they didn't even know what their needs were! They were caught in the cycle of endless giving to others.

So we began coaching adults. In the process, we discovered ways to better recognize our own needs, activate a cycle of receiving, and really go for what we want! Here are the Three Secrets we discovered:

1. Personal needs must come first.
2. You are in charge of making sure you get what you need.
3. You can give to and receive from yourself.

You might be thinking, "I don't have time for personal needs. Remember? The need for more time leads the list at the beginning of this chapter! If I had more time, I could accomplish my career goals, make more money, and have more balance in my life." Well, we're not so sure. As women, we know a lot about giving, but unless we learn about receiving, we'll just use that extra time giving more. . . and be back in the same old cycle.

What we are sure about is this: unless you figure out what you need, *personally*, to feel content and at peace, career goals, relationship goals, and the balance you are craving, won't happen. We have noticed when the two of us step back and honor our deep, personal needs, our business moves forward and more of our career goals are reached.

So, what do we advise women to stop the endless cycle of giving and start getting as much as they give? Here are the Three Steps we teach in our Power of You Now!™ Seminars:

1. Let go of your 'Mistaken Identity'
2. Embrace your 'True Identity'
3. Give yourself what you need and want

1. LET GO OF YOUR MISTAKEN IDENTITY

Did you know that most of us grow up under a Mistaken Identity? Mistaken Identities result from negative, inaccurate labels and judgments people make about us when we are young, and we tend to internalize these myths as the truth. They are powerful, controlling beliefs that dictate what we should and shouldn't be thinking, saying and doing; because of them, we judge ourselves as bad, wrong, or unworthy, which is the major roadblock to getting what we need.

Many of these internalized myths originate from our school experiences. Although teachers have the best of intentions, many students conclude they are failures or at least, "just average." These beliefs can control us for our entire lives.

It is essential to let go of your Mistaken Identity and learn the truth about who you are. Your future happiness and success depend upon it.

Here are examples of myths you might have grown up with:
- I have to give 100% to everything I do.
- If I don't go to college, I won't get anywhere.
- I'll never make it. . . (as an artist, musician, firefighter, etc. . .)

Here are examples of truths to replace the old myths:
- Comparison with others creates dust on my brilliance.
- I get to decide what's important to me.
- Interests are the greatest motivators. I'll do what I love!

Here are examples of common mis-labels with a new truth next to each:
- I'm only average.
- I ask too many questions.
- I'm a daydreamer.

- I have my own areas of brilliance.
- I am curious and inventive.
- I need time to think things out.

Let go of your Mistaken Identity and embrace your True Identity, by making your own list of truths about yourself and reading it several times a day.

2. EMBRACE YOUR TRUE IDENTITY

Like many women who strive for self-improvement, you have probably learned from dozens of speakers and authors that you *should* make time for yourself: journal writing, bubble baths, power gym workouts, etc. In addition, you are *supposed* to set aside time for your hobbies, talks with your significant other, playing with your kids, developing business goals, and just relaxing!

It all sounds good when you're listening to that dynamic speaker, but then you go back to the real world and figure—none of this is possible in my life. *Could it be that you don't really want many of these things?* When embracing your True Identity, the first question to ask is, "What do I actually want?" There's no such thing as what you are *supposed* to want!

Eliminating all the things you *don't* want often brings great relief. Whatever they may be—talking in front of groups, doing the dishes, journal writing, making sales calls—just erase them from your "supposed to" list! You hate bookkeeping? Fine, find someone who loves to do that part. You're not the organizing type? Great! You come up with the ideas and have someone else organize.

To begin to embrace your True Identity—the *real you*—make a list of what you need and want:

- Yes, that bubble bath is for me!
- I need 30 minutes of quiet time every morning!
- I will attend only one game a month with my sports-loving family—at other times I will go to a quiet park and write poetry!

If you are used to thinking about the needs of others, it can be difficult to think about your own needs. However, when you reconnect with your needs, you rekindle your spirit to take action on your behalf—to get what you need and want. Enjoy knowing the truth about you! Celebrate who you are!

3. GIVE YOURSELF WHAT YOU NEED AND WANT.

Now that you know who you are and what you want, you are likely to feel more content and peaceful. The happier you are with YOU, the more likely it is that you will want to take care of your needs—to give yourself "gifts." The more at peace you are with YOU, the more you will be able to receive these gifts.

Choose just one thing that you need and *give it to yourself!* Make a step-by-step plan for how to bring it into your life. As you give yourself more and more gifts and more of your personal needs are met, you will be surprised to see the positive changes in your life.

So if you've ever wondered if it's possible to get what you want, our message to you is, *Yes, it is possible!* The Three Secrets and Three Steps we've shared are helping us day by day to get more of what we want and to help our clients do the same.

Begin using the Three Secrets and Three Steps today to start you on your way to receiving as much as you give, and achieving more of what YOU really want in your life!

VICTORIA KINDLE HODSON, M.A. AND MARIAEMMA PELULLO-WILLIS, M.S. are authors, speakers and success coaches. They are co-founders of the Learning-Success™ Institute and Power of You Now!™ Seminars. Published works include the best-selling book, "Discover Your Child's Learning Style." For more information, go to www.powerofyounow.com. To find out more about your own learning and working styles go to www.aselfportraitonline.com. Learning-Success™ Institute: 1590 E. Main St., Ventura, CA 93001 Victoria: v@learningsuccesscoach.com, 805-653-0261. Mariaemma: m@learningsuccesscoach.com, 805-648-1739.

CHAPTER 9

The Wise Women's Guide To Eating Well

JEANNE PETERS

DO YOU FEEL TOTALLY CONFUSED by what kind of diet to follow—Low carb. . . Hi protein. . . Low fat? Do you spend more time re-charging your cell phone than re-charging your body's basic needs? Would you like to make peace with food and diets once and for all?

If you answered yes to any or all of these questions, you are not alone. For many of us women, food is a source of conflict and confusion rather than a source of true nourishment. We feel overwhelmed by the never-ending search for the "the best eating system". We obsess about our weight, cravings and body image. We eat on the run, divide food into "good" and " bad" categories, and then punish ourselves for making the wrong choices. We yearn to return to the times when eating well was a simple and pleasurable experience. I know. As a Registered Dietitian in practice for over 25 years, I have counseled and spoken to thousands of women in all stages of life. . . puberty, pregnancy, peri-menopause and menopause. And the question that often arises is, what should I eat. . . or what's missing in my diet? And this question speaks to something much deeper that is missing in our diet—something needed beyond another supplement or diet plan.

In my search for an integrated eating approach amid all the conflicting theories, I realized what's missing in our current dietary systems and approaches is a lack of spiritual connections with food; the body and the earth that provides our source of nourishment. In traditional cultures throughout history, ancient people's survival was dependent upon their being stewards of the earth. To raise, gather and prepare food was an honored and respected daily ritual. People lived in tune with the seasonal rhythms and created celebrations and feasts to honor their labors and the abundance of the earth.

In our busy modern culture, we often forget our survival is still dependent upon the Earth, and yet most of us have very little connection with our food sources. This loss is having an impact upon our health and our spirits. The experience of eating provides so much more than fuel for the physical body. In my work, I encourage clients to consider all the other factors which are equally significant in determining whether a meal is truly nourishing: The less tangible "ingredients" of a meal, such as the source of our food, the consciousness with which it is eaten, as well as the ambiance of our surroundings, and the people in whose company we dine. These are all part of the nourishing experience, and they profoundly affect the body and mind at physical and subtle energetic levels. Clients who enroll in my *Wise Women Eat Well Cookshops,* learn how to cultivate awareness and confidence in their inherent body wisdom. This skill allows women to tune in and determine for themselves the types of food that best meet their individual needs. It requires rigor and commitment. And yet the payoff is never having to diet again!

Here are a few eating principles that if practiced regularly, can help you eat well and create a healthier relationship with food.

PRACTICE NUTRITIONAL SELF CARE

This is about taking care of one of our most basic needs—eating. Most women do not eat enough during the day. They skip breakfast; grab a light lunch of yogurt or salad. Even if you have an afternoon snack, by dinner you end up ravenous. Since you've been "good" all day, you start rummaging through the pantry and fridge. But no matter what or how much you eat, you can't quite suppress your hunger. If you get too hungry, all intentions of moderate, conscious eating fly out the window. The problem with ignoring your feelings of hunger is you also start ignoring your feelings of fullness. Soon your body isn't in control of your eating—your diet is. Skipping meals and snacks is a set up to binge or overeat. Try to tune into hunger and eat shortly after noticing hunger. To maintain an adequate blood sugar level so you don't become too hungry, it is important to eat regularly.

Eating regularly means:
- Eat 4 to 6 smaller, nutritionally dense meals instead of three large ones.
- Balance meals and snacks with lean protein and high fiber carbohydrates like veggies
- Space meals no more than 3 to 5 hours apart.

PRACTICE MINDFULNESS WHEN EATING

In many spiritual disciplines and religious traditions, there are a variety of ways that conscious eating is practiced. Blessings and rituals are performed before and while meals are eaten. What practice can you integrate into your lifestyle that would serve to enrich your relationship with food?

Enhance your environment by turning off the TV, arrange the dining table with candles and flowers for beauty, and take a few deep breaths prior to eating to center yourself in the present moment.

Consider giving thanks for all the energy that went into creating the meal. This allows us to feel the interconnectedness with the world that contributes to our nourishment.

Begin by eating a little slower. This will help you savor the flavors of food you eat. The more time and attention you give to food, the more satisfying the experience. Through certain mindful exercises, we can develop the body's intuitive wisdom to determine which foods would be most nourishing at a given time.

EAT A VARIETY OF FRESH, WHOLE UNPROCESSED FOODS AS OFTEN AS POSSIBLE.

Lastly, be sure to keep an abundance and variety of good wholesome foods. Wise women eat this way because it increases the chances of getting all 50 of the nutrients needed for optimal nutrition. Reward yourself with nutritious food, which leaves you feeling energized and alive. Fill your house with all sorts of enjoyable fresh foods—seasonal fruits and vegetables, beans, whole grains, lean meats, poultry, fish and dairy products.

Start today with one small step.

Go beyond those common baby carrots and try something new like beets or Swiss chard or a kiwi for fruit. Trying one new food each week could be the beginning of an adventurous and healthy relationship with food.

These are just three simple principles that are part of one whole integrated eating system to enhance a women's physical, emotional and spiritual well-being. Recently, at the conclusion of a Wise Women Eat Well seminar, a group of women responded to the question, "What and how do wise women eat?" Here are their thoughts to chew on.

- Wise Women distinguish the difference between physical hunger and the urge to eat to satisfy some other unmet need
- Wise Women eat with fun and spontaneity and learn to trust their inner wisdom
- Wise Women eat to be fulfilled instead of filling up
- Wise Women eat with all of their senses, enjoying the textures, flavors, sensuous aromas, and the palette of healing wholesome foods
- Wise women offer appreciation for the food they eat
- Wise women eat for true nourishment

Make a commitment to yourself to discover how to eat in a way that truly nourishes all parts of your being. Our bodies know what they need, if we learn to listen to them. Reconnecting to that wisdom, and honoring it with wholesome food choices are needed steps towards healing our bodies. Feeling vitalized from this form of self-care will give you the energy to fuel your daily life and your significant dreams.

JEANNE PETERS R.D. is dedicated to helping women heal and nourish their body, mind and spirits through her popular Wise Women Eat Well cookshops, teleseminars and individualized counseling. She loves sharing her integrated lifestyle approach to cooking, eating, and weight management with women of all ages. Her mission is to transform our cultural food crisis into the possibility of true nourishment. She can be reached at: www.nourishingwellness.com; e-mail at eat4hlthrd@aol.com; phone at 310-795-7668.

CHAPTER 10

Finding Your Dream Job

Discovering Your Purpose &
Living Your Passion In Life

HEATHER REM

HOW WOULD IT FEEL if you didn't have to work hard? What if your life and work were effortless and fun the majority of the time? What if you got up in the morning feeling energized and ready to go to work because you love what you do every day? What if you had the ability to create your reality around your work environment, salary, amount of hours you work and type of people you work with?

This may seem impossible to you because this is not naturally the way we are brought up to think. While growing up, most of us have heard work is hard—it's about making a living. We go to school to get a degree, which will enable us to get a good job, and then make as much money as possible. In fact, we are discouraged to become a writer, an actor or an artist, and we are told we could never make a living by pursuing a career like that. No one ever asks us what feels easy, effortless and fun in our lives and encourages us to pursue that as a career.

To find your Dream Job, you will have to let go of this old way of thinking. I am well aware most of us live in our comfort zone;

moving out of it can be a very scary proposition. Internally, we are used to being a certain way or thinking a certain way and even if this way isn't working for us, we stick with it because it's comfortable. It's what we know. Living passionately means stretching beyond this comfort zone to reach your dreams and goals. It is uncomfortable at first, but the payoff is well worth it.

Many of my clients come to me with the desire to make a career change; many use the phrase, "I want to find my passion." I encourage them to begin this process by seeking to discover their true purpose in life. This is the first step towards becoming passionate about your work and loving what you do every day. I believe that work should be as effortless as possible. My philosophy is if it's a struggle, you probably aren't working in your Dream Job or living your true passion.

One way to find your purpose in life is to recognize your values. By discovering and embracing your values, you will find yourself in the "flow" of life, where everything is easier and seems to make sense. No matter what challenges you encounter or curveballs you are thrown, if you live your life aligned with your values on a daily basis, you will find your life will always have meaning. Knowing your values allows you to have a deep understanding of "why you are here." Below are some exercises to start the process of discovering your purpose and passion in life:

- *Values are things you feel connected to; they allow you to feel peaceful inside, and truly alive.*
  Make a list of 4 or 5 core values that are important to you. Some examples of values are: to be Adventurous, Daring, Honest, Elegant, to Contribute, Teach, Create, Discover, Learn, Experience, Feel, Lead, Inspire, Master, Excel, Pleasure, to Have Fun, to Relate, to be Connected, Sensitive, Supportive, Spiritual, to Instruct, Uplift, Win, Accomplish, Acquire.
- *Look at your life and see where your values currently show up and in what ways.*

As an example, my core value is connecting with people and helping them to move forward in their lives. When I discovered this and began to look at my life/my previous jobs, etc. I realized I had been in some way incorporating this value into my daily life. When I acknowledged how important this was to me, I began the process of discovering what I could do for a career that would purely honor this value. As a coach, I am engaged in my purpose everyday and my life is filled with joy, ease and a feeling of fulfillment.

- *After you have chosen your core values, practice honoring them by orienting your life and your choices around them.*
  If a value for you is to teach or to inspire and you are working in a computer company doing data entry, isolated and never interacting with anyone all day, you may want to think about making a job change that incorporates your core value. Either that or start volunteering with a charity.

After you have established your values, the next step is to discover what you love to do. The next three exercises will help you in this process:

- Make a list of your past jobs and what elements felt most right. What excited you most, put a smile on your face, felt effortless and fun?
- What do you love to do in your free time? What do you consider a hobby that you have never considered getting paid for because it is too much fun, too easy, or it revolved around helping others? Usually this is just the thing you can turn into your Dream Job. I had a client that helped all of her friends faux finish their homes. She was always helping and teaching them how to make their homes beautiful. When we were trying to discover her Dream Job and I mentioned this to her, she said she

couldn't imagine getting paid for helping others beautify their homes because it was so easy and fun! Why not get paid to do what you love and are passionate about?

- Now look back at your childhood and think about what you loved to do as a kid, or what you wanted to be when you were little; this dream that faded away or some skill you are aware of might be the key to your Dream Job. I had a client who wanted to change careers and remembered as a kid he loved to throw parties for the neighborhood. He now successfully works as a Corporate Event Planner.

You now have the tools to take a step towards your future and finding your Dream Job. Take baby steps to begin with; live your purpose on a daily basis, and watch how effortless life becomes. When you are authentic and know what makes you feel happy and alive, you are not afraid of what people will think of you when you go for your dreams.

Recognize that life is a journey, and what makes it passionate is not the end result, but the experience you have getting there. Living life for the enjoyment you receive from it each day and knowing you are committed to your dream, is a powerful way to feel enriched and passionate.

After I discovered my purpose and passion in life was coaching others, I asked myself where I could get support to make my dream a reality. I surrounded myself with people who respected my choices, who encouraged me to "go for it," and I hired a coach to assist me in the process of building my business, move through my fears and celebrate my wins. Support is a key factor in this process. Find a mentor, a coach, someone who is living life passionately and on purpose. Set yourself up to succeed by creating a plan and system to help you while you make the necessary changes in thought and action to begin to live a passionate life.

HEATHER REM of InnerPower Coaching is a Personal Transition Coach working with individuals in career and life transition. She coaches her clients to accomplish their goals, conquer their fears and move forward in their lives. She was the Director of Entertainment Marketing and Celebrity Relations for Reebok and has worked with creative people in the entertainment industry for fourteen years. For more information about "Finding Your Dream Job Workshop" call 818-755-1797 or visit Heather at www.innerpowercoaching.com.

CHAPTER 11

Movie Star Parking In A Minimum Wage World

MELISSA ROSE, C.Ht.

Space. . . the final frontier.
—Star Trek

IS SPACE TRULY THE FINAL FRONTIER, or is it simply overrated? After all, why should we get caught up in our universe when our own world provides us with so many challenges? Many of us spend the majority of our busy lives bumping around from one project to the next, hoping life will provide us with the perfect job, situation or relationship. This seems perfectly reasonable, however, rooted within this behavior is something most of us are not aware of.

Consider the possibility that we might just be passing time because we are too afraid to listen and then carry out what our inner voice pleads for us to do. Often, our commitment towards family, friends and work serve to overshadow, and in some cases, undermine our dreams.

After all, with so many external responsibilities, how can we possibly have the time needed to become personally successful? Even a little dream seems overwhelming when the laundry is piling up in the corner of your bedroom. Certainly, I'm not suggesting we disregard every day responsibilities. What I am saying is . . . wouldn't the greater good be better served if more dreams came true?

How many people do you think watch the Academy Awards and imagine what it would be like to accept such a prestigious award, to be recognized and appreciated for their talent and abilities? Yet, how many people actually take a step towards that amazing possibility? Proportionately, few will ever have the confidence to pursue such a dream. Many of us are content to stay rooted in our daily routine simply because it is comfortable.

Are we in agreement? Or are you about ready to move on to the next chapter?

In the first case, you may now be realizing you need a change in your life; in the latter, you may be among those too inhibited to take the first step. In either case, I urge you to consider taking a baby step toward a fulfilling lifestyle. The rewards you reap in the process, and over time, will be richly satisfying! And who among us couldn't use a bit more satisfaction in our lives?

There are many things you can do to help create positive flow in your life. Believe it or not, many of these tools take no more than a few seconds of your time. Yet, when applied daily, these techniques will help you feel happier and more content.

Yes, it's true. . . No more staying up all night watching your favorite infomercials just to take your mind off the worries from your day.

THE FIRST STEP TOWARDS YOUR MOVIE STAR LIFESTYLE IS "ATTITUDE."

To determine what kind of attitude you have, try dedicating a day toward observing your own behavior. Pay attention to how you react to every day circumstances.

How do you handle your stressors? What kind of mood are you in most of the time? How do you feel about yourself? Are you spending too much time wondering what other people think about you? Are you letting your need to please others rule how you get through your day?

Think of yourself as a research project and find out what makes you tick. Then do something with the information. If you take this baby step, you will start to identify the unique rituals and patterns that rule your daily routine.

Concentrate on one reaction or pattern at a time, and then think about how to change it. For example, if you are guilty of spending too much time wondering about things that may or may not happen, then practice the following technique: stop the thought when it occurs; then relanguage the thought immediately into something more positive and constructive.

Let's say you are meeting somebody for the first time and are uncomfortable with how the first few minutes of conversation have gone. Stop and give yourself a boost by calling on your inner movie star. You're probably familiar with the famous theater mantra "The show must go on," which simply suggests no matter what happens, you cannot stop and rewind.

Have fun with this game! In your world the curtain has gone up; the conversation has begun, and you must continue despite how awkward things may have started.

Create an alter ego for your inner movie star and remember your inner movie star needs to have her chance in the limelight in order to perform and shine.

Self-talk varies from person to person. Typically, people can be pretty hard on themselves. One way to cut through the negative self-talk is to learn to praise yourself for the little things you do. By emphasizing the positive aspects of your life and appreciating what you have, your self-talk will slowly change from a focus of "lack" to one of "abundance." It is another form of attitude adjustment.

Basically, most people appreciate their family and friends and maybe a handful of other things, but our inner accomplishments tend to go unnoticed. Begin learning to appreciate yourself by taking small steps.

Start by recognizing your daily accomplishments. Give yourself a pat on the back for every achievement whether it is something big or small. For example: you have always wanted to exercise daily, but for some reason you can't seem to do it. Celebrate every day you do exercise and don't react to the days you don't. Accept yourself unconditionally. Applaud your imperfections.

Celebrate the first day you do something hard. . . don't wait until you do it for a month. Let your inner movie star have a night out on the town. Everyone is different so don't beat yourself up. Most of all, don't compare yourself to others. Consistently, give yourself the encouragement you would give a good friend or a child. Once you master appreciation for yourself, then you are ready to take yourself less seriously.

Humor is one of the greatest equalizers. Instead of putting yourself down, find humor in your actions. If you don't find any humor in the fact that you have certain rituals, then take yourself to a funny movie or see a great stand up comedy revue.

The first thing you will notice is that you are laughing because you identify with their stories. Their stories are our stories, and as we start to take ourselves less seriously, we can start laughing at what we think are our inadequacies. Once this shift occurs and you start to laugh at those dark little secrets, they don't seem as powerful and you can start to let go and break out of the rut.

Humor can help you acknowledge your discomfort while arming you with the boost you might need to get through an uncomfortable or comfortable situation that previously you would have avoided out of fear. Utilizing self-laughter will give you choices.

Your days of feeling paralyzed with "what if" scenarios will be in the past; this will allow new, healthier patterns to emerge. Nothing is ever as bad as you think it might be. Your inner movie star can work miracles in your life if you let her.

The more you practice these techniques, the easier difficult scenarios will become. Remember—it's your turn to shine. Let the spotlight in and take a bow. You are the star of your life, and you are the leading lady who deserves the Academy Award for best performance in a life well lived! This moment is yours, and your limousine is waiting. . . All you have to do now is, enjoy the ride.

MELISSA ROSE is a Certified Clinical Hypnotherapist and best selling author of the CD: Overcoming Obstacles; a self-hypnosis journey for unlocking creativity, self-confidence and self-esteem. Melissa holds a BA in Business and Economics from the University of California, Santa Barbara. Her synergy of intuition and skill along with her background in business and hypnotherapy supplies both creative and analytical personalities with the skills they need to flourish. For more information email Melissa at: hypnoforu@aol.com

CHAPTER 12

The Superwoman Juggling Act

DR. YVONNE THOMAS, Ph.D.

IN THIS FAST-PACED, ADVANCED TECHNOLOGY-WORLD we live in, life can seem more complicated and stressful than ever before. Along with all the roles and tasks in which we participate, there are also e-mails, voice-mails, cell phones, and the Internet to stay on top of. It is a "Superwoman juggling act" trying to keep up with, let alone have time for, all parts of our lives.

The original Chaka Khan song, "I'm Every Woman," seems most appropriate for many of us! However, while productivity, multi-tasking, and completing things on your "to-do" list can be very rewarding, the juggling act needs to stop sometimes so you can actually enjoy and partake in life. Here are several important steps you can utilize to gain more control over your juggling act and not "drop the ball" on your happiness.

Through my years of helping clients make life changes, I have found it is important to make your goal "concrete" and "visual" so you can literally see where things currently are and where you want them to be. I suggest creating a "pie chart" to indicate the various areas of your life. Areas should include: significant others, friends, work, family-of-origin (parents, siblings, etc.), children, physical and emotional health, religion/spirituality, hobbies, etc. Be sure to include "time for self" as well.

Next, note the percentages each of your life areas typically receives and what you would like each area to optimally get. Then, display this chart in a place where you'll see it daily and use it as an ongoing tool and reminder to keep you structured and concretely aware of all your key life parts.

Additionally, try to live your life in accordance with the priority and value you've assigned each of these parts. Here is a helpful technique I use with clients. Imagine that you are at the end of your life looking back, and then ask yourself, "What areas do I wish I had devoted more time and attention to?" Once you are at the end of your life, it's too late to change such things. So, grab the opportunity now to make your life what you want it to be and end up with the fewest regrets possible.

Furthermore, remember that nothing is perfect, so tailor your self-expectations to a realistic human level when creating your daily "to-do" list and do not expect to complete everything, let alone to do it all flawlessly! Many people believe if they do things perfectly in their lives, they will be happy, stress-free people. The ironic truth is attempting to reach and maintain perfection is actually a stress-inducing way to live life driven by impossible standards.

Too often, when a person strives for perfection and doesn't get it, she may end up feeling bad about herself overall, rather than just about that specific area. Ultimately, it is critical to remember: being perfect isn't what matters—being balanced with a well-rounded, meaningful, fulfilled life is. Thus, give yourself credit for what you were able to accomplish on a given day and recognize that your "mere mortal," non-Superhuman efforts actually may be "good enough."

In addition, creating balance includes being able to say "no." You must draw boundaries and back them up so your actions match your words. This is important! It helps you respect yourself by valuing and preserving all those areas of your life that matter to you. As I tell my clients, "Avoid having mixed messages" which invalidate your point and leave the recipient of your message confused.

Also, be aware that one should not feel guilty for saying "no" and/or setting boundaries; these are healthy, self-respecting behaviors to help you regulate your time and your priorities.

Furthermore, it is important to be realistic with time. Consider how long it will likely take to complete a task, to drive and stay somewhere, etc. Since there are only 24 hours in a day, people can underestimate how long it may actually take to do things; they may not adequately plan for traffic, unexpected interruptions, weather, etc. Try to pad the day with some time that is unscheduled so if you run longer than expected with something, you may still end up being on time for your next "to-do."

Finally, recognize the "wear and tear" effects of being the nonstop Superwoman. Most likely, if you are one of these women, you either don't have or take much time to determine the high price you may be paying. Over the years, I have provided therapy to many women like this. They have all been amazingly "talented" at keeping their juggling acts going; some even have been additionally "gifted" with the ability to keep adding more balls to juggle.

The reasons are diverse as to why one may take on this Superwoman gig (i.e., issues related to overachieving, perfectionism, workaholism, never feeling good enough, or simply because one genuinely does have an overabundance of simultaneous responsibilities and tasks, etc.). No matter what the reasons may be, none of my clients are happy living this way.

Although you as the Superwoman may accomplish more in a day than most people, perhaps you are not getting the sleep, exercise, nutrition, and downtime we all really need. The lack of having these foundational elements in place can cause both physical and emotional difficulties.

Negative physical consequences include: suffering from over- or under-eating, not being physically fit and healthy, often being tired or even exhausted, looking more haggard and older than you really are, and/or frequently getting sick since you are chronically worn out.

Negative emotional consequences can occur since you probably don't take the time or opportunity to feel as often as you should. This creates a backlog of unexpressed emotions which can accumulate into depression, anxiety, and/or stress. Other negative emotional ramifications include: low self-esteem, irritability, impatience, and lack of closeness in relationships with people, including your significant other and your children, since you don't have the time to have a quality relationship.

However, change is possible! Specifically include in some of your "me time" ways to minimize and counteract some of the "Superwoman juggling act" effects. Do things to reinvigorate and nurture your soul (i.e., listen to music that is uplifting or personally meaningful, have calming scents like vanilla or cinnamon around you, and create outlets for stress-reduction such as regularly-scheduled exercise, yoga, etc.).

Also, try to build self-nurturing basics back into your life with healthy amounts of eating, sleeping, regular contact with supportive family and friends, creativity, and laughter as a way to occasionally "lighten up." In conjunction with this, give yourself a "to-do" of taking a few minutes a day to just breath, take stock of, and appreciate all you have in your life, because what are you doing it all for anyway?

And periodically shake things up by getting off the "non-stop treadmill" and experiment with things you haven't tried before. By doing this occasionally, it will help you break out of the constantly moving Superwoman cycle while broadening your world and your personal growth.

The bottom line is juggling less rather than more can make you a much calmer, more efficient, productive, lovable, and confident woman who can be happy and healthy without all the "balls" and whistles!

With three Psychology degrees, wisdom, and warmth, licensed Psychologist YVONNE THOMAS, PH.D. has enjoyed a successful, Los Angeles private practice since 1988. Her specialties include relation-ships, body-image, self-esteem, perfectionism, overeating, life transi-tions, anxiety, and depression. Dr. Thomas is frequently interviewed and quoted as a Media Psychologist for radio, TV, magazines, and newspapers. Her expertise is extensively showcased in "Unblemished" (Simon and Schuster, 2004) by Drs. Katie Rodan and Kathy Fields. She currently writes for two publications. Call 310-726-3944 or see www.dryvonnethomas.com or www.yvonnethomasphd.com

CHAPTER 13

Powerful, Purposeful Living

Awareness + Choice + Responsibility = Power

VERONICA CRYSTAL YOUNG

THE PERSONAL CREED I attempt to live my life by is "Responsibility of choice is the BE to life." I have found great power and liberation in this statement. While some I share my motto with grab onto it wholeheartedly, others have found it powerfully upsetting. I attribute my success in the medical field and my creative endeavors in the entertainment field to this "Power" equation.

We live in a world where outside influences permeate all areas of our lives. Most of us juggle to find a balance between the elements of our inner being with what we have to accomplish in the outer world. Media campaigns, ranging from the Pharmaceutical company's best drug for your loneliness to Madison Avenue's acceptable body image, sometime leave us with unrealistic expectations of others and ourselves. We truly are an other's society, where our views and feelings about who we are, can easily be defined by another. Being fully present is a delicate balancing act of self-awareness and "other" awareness.

Through the years people have said knowledge is power. Consciousness is knowledge of self. When we are self aware, we see we have choices in each and every situation. So many of us have come from less than ideal circumstances and have tales of childhood abuse, uncaring parents, lack of money or formal education. Of course these circumstances, among many others, can make self-awareness and consciousness of choice extremely difficult to maintain in the face of low self-esteem, anger or an almost broken spirit. When we fully realize we actually have distinct choices in each and every situation, we free ourselves from a trajectory of victim-based or other-based choices.

We are challenged in our lives by many choices each day, some seemingly inconsequential. We are challenged by our senses, by what feels good and our own expectations. It is in the choices that we consciously, and unfortunately unconsciously make, that we define who we are. It is in the choices we make that the "we" is revealed to others and ourselves.

How many times have we done something because it felt good, only to dread it afterward? Was the dread from our own expectations unfulfilled? Was it from our guilt about how we acted in the situation or how we looked or defined ourselves by making that choice? Awareness is 20/20 in hindsight, but consistently having the courage and awareness to reveal who we really are through our choices can truly be a powerful way to live.

One day I had a strong enough desire to look honestly at the reasons my life was not working. Talk about a freeing day! I found my way to healing and forgiveness as a choice. Painful though it was, I had to admit my personal situation existed solely because of the previous choices I felt I *had* to make. Of course there were always other choices to make, but "other" choices were not who I wanted to be at the time. Then I found I needed to make yet another choice, one to consciously make the decision to go deeply into my own psyche when faced with any choices; to walk awake and find the energy to face myself and the impact my choices have.

Just as an example, here are my litmus test questions for choices: Will this intentionally hurt anyone? If so, how well can I live with it, and can I live knowing who I am because of it? Will this make me unpopular or popular with my boss, husband, wife, partner, child? Will I be defined by a possible unpopularity or by the power of my choice? Am I responsible for others' feelings about me or mine? Do I care? If so, why? This may seem elementary but upon true, deep self-examination, we have to be honest with ourselves to grasp the root of our reasons for certain choices. You may discover your choices have nothing to do with you at all, and everything to do with the roles you play. And it is at this point you must decide if a choice is in line with who you wish to be.

Once I had deepened my understanding of choice, I had to accept the responsibility that came with those choices; all choices. Responsibility goes beyond committed action. It includes acceptance of consequences, and it also includes a responsibility to self and who we want to BE. One way of looking at it is, what is our commitment to the choice, i.e. what is our "response" ability? Again, will we be able to live with our choice? Will it reflect who we want to be? If not, maybe another choice would be the better choice.

One thing I had to develop was patience. Patience is like permission to take time for self-discovery. I had to make the commitment of taking time to discover my reasons for past choices, how they impacted my life, and I had to do this by myself. In the beginning, I could only accomplish this kind of consciousness alone. To bring another into the equation early on would have meant my focus would be on them, not me. So, I would take a weekend or an evening and just sit by the ocean or somewhere in nature, and just listen. Listen to the chatter in my head, the questions and the answers, because you know I had both! It was quite noisy in my head sometimes!

At first it was a bit frightening to look at my life in "choice snapshots," but the ultimate goal was to weed out those beliefs I had taken on from other significant people in my life. Parents, church, peers, husband, children, and society. All had an enormous amount of influence over the reasons I had taken particular paths. It was then a joy to fully realize I was at choice yet again. I had to decide if my past reasons would continue to define who I was, or if I would fully commit to who *I had become* and make more powerful choices based on my fully realized reasons.

It continues to be a challenge to identify and dissect each option and choice on a daily basis. I have found that taking those little self-discovery trips on a quarterly basis does wonders for my psyche and my sanity! I head for that beach and listen to the waves ebb and flow, and it brings me to center every time. My center, my "Being". Take the time to find the *goddess*, or the *god-essence* within. Find your spirit-center; find awareness of your "self."

It was in my complete awareness of self and choice, that I found my own personal power. I invite you to choose a course of action that is true to your selves and take responsibility for the choice(s) that will ultimately allow you to live a powerful, purposeful life.

VERONICA CRYSTAL YOUNG is President of Crystal Eyes Entertainment and creator of TV ArtScapes, a powerful DVD series that allows you to replenish your spirit by creating an atmosphere of tranquility at home or at work. She is also a consultant for Medical Practice Management. Affiliations/Board Positions: National Association for Female Executives (NAFE); Women Inc; AFTRA; NRDC; Co-Op America; Women in Theatre; Broadway on Sunset; Theatre of Hope; Arts Advocacy Commission. 310-842-6001 tvartscapes@aol.com www.tvartscapes.com

PART II

BUSINESS AND FINANCIAL

FULFILLMENT

CHAPTER 14

How The Millionaire Next Door Can Be You

MERI ANNE BECK-WOODS

Chairman & CFO, Odyssey Advisors, LLC

TO A YOUNG PERSON, a million dollars sounds like a lot of money. To someone approaching retirement, it may not seem like enough, especially if they want to live comfortably for the rest of their life.

Most well-known evangelists in the church of making money will tell you the best way to get rich is to save and invest 10% to 15% of your income by automatically deducting it from your salary or other earnings before you begin to pay your bills. These people are charismatic, enthusiastic, and oftentimes knowledgeable. They are also trying to sell you something. The product is usually a book, a CD, a "proven" method or mind-set that will help you achieve your goal of becoming a millionaire. These people know if they can motivate you to save that amount, simple compound interest will act in your favor and eventually make you a millionaire. If you are inspired to actually save and invest that much, whatever the cost of the motivation, it is probably well worth it.

I have been working since I was 12 years old. I am older now, however I *choose* to work; I don't have to. I was a mini-entrepreneur and sold greeting cards and stationery door-to-door when the world was a safer place for such activity. Growing up, my family was constantly moving from place to place and as a result, I attended 18 different grammar schools. But I learned the valuable lesson "To adapt to changing circumstances." This is also essential to becoming a millionaire, as asset allocation among different investment choices is the most important factor that determines both your risk and return.

Everyone has it in them to become a millionaire. It does not matter who your parents were or how they treated you, where you went to school, what you look like, or where you live. Those things might help you get to a million dollars faster, but in the end all that matters is how you and others value what you do, what form that value takes, and how you choose to make it grow.

A set of studies by *Ibbotson and Sinquefield* details historical returns among the major asset classes since 1926; each year they publish a yearbook updating the data. These studies showed stocks of smaller companies had higher returns than larger companies at 12.5% vs. 10.5%; intermediate-term bonds had higher returns and less risk than 20-year bonds by a marginal amount, and Treasury Bills had the lowest return with the least amount of risk.

The longer you have to save and invest, the greater the potential for becoming a millionaire. The main reason the returns were higher for certain asset classes, was because they involved greater risk measured either by price change or risk of loss. Also, how soon you plan to retire, go to college or buy a house makes a difference. If you have a long time horizon, you can weather a downturn in stocks and afford to keep invested for the recovery. So, the younger you are, the more stocks you can have in your portfolio.

As you age and accumulate more wealth, you have more to lose so bonds become a greater part of your investments. This lessens the risk of your portfolio but also lessens the return. Benjamin Franklin said, "If a man empties his purse into his head no one can take it away from him. An investment in knowledge always pays the best interest." I believe this goes for women as well. So learning to adapt, and becoming knowledgeable or expert in any given field will aid in your journey to be a millionaire. It's about wisdom gained through experience and searching. It is not always about getting the highest degree in school, since degrees and certifications sometimes become barriers to entry or union cards to lessen competition.

Use your energy to learn what you need to know and where to find that information. If you are an entrepreneur, you want to sell a product or perform a service that solves a problem, provides benefit, and is in demand at a price that will create a profit. A good Internet site is www.Entrepreneur.com. For women in particular, www.newentrepreneurs.com is excellent for networking, to cross-refer, and build your business. If you want to start an investment club in order to exchange ideas and pool your resources with others, you can go to www.i-sophia.com and get an investment club kit and sign up for a financial education newsletter. The Internet is an invaluable resource for getting an on-line education, researching companies and industries you want to work for or invest in, as well as giving you access to hundreds of articles written by experts in various professions.

One big misconception many people have is if they don't have a lot of money they cannot save money, let alone invest—NOT SO! If you are unable to make the maximum IRA or 401K contribution or don't have thousands of dollars to invest in stocks or make a down payment on a home, you still can become the millionaire you dream about by saving and investing regularly. Whether that means dumping your spare change into a jar or contributing to a low-cost fund purchase plan, getting an interest only, or no down payment mortgage, doing it, and getting into the habit, can make the difference in whether you succeed in becoming a millionaire or not.

If you want to be a millionaire, you need to ask yourself some questions. How much sleep do you want to get at night while getting there? Do you think you invest to win, or do you want to invest not to lose? There is a significant difference in how you achieve your goal depending on your answer to that question. Warren Buffett says, "Invest in what you know." He followed his own advice and avoided the stock market technology bubble in the late 90s. Since then, Buffett's Berkshire Hathaway holdings have gone from 73% stocks and 21% bonds in 1997 to only 26% stocks, 35% bonds and 30% operating companies in 2003.

An alternate path to becoming a millionaire is to sell a company you have grown to another party (preferably not Warren Buffett because he does not pay retail). Small business owners are starting companies now more than ever before. The virtual office, outsourcing of human resources, payroll and bookkeeping can give someone an 8-foot commute instead of an hour. More and more small companies have low-cost advantages that allow them to compete with much larger competitors.

The person who wants to sleep tight every night can become a millionaire by paying off their home mortgage, keeping a zero balance on their credit cards, living modestly and putting even more income into things like dividend-paying stocks that provide growing income and a tax advantage (since the dividends are taxed at 15% these days). To find out more information about these kinds of stocks, *Value Line* has a listing of "**147 Stocks That Increased Their Dividends Every Year For the Past 10 Years.**"

When I managed money for Norton Simon and his wife actress Jennifer Jones, she wanted to buy a Rolls Royce. He said "no" and bought her a Cadillac station wagon. It was cheaper, and the back of the car was big enough to transport his priceless paintings. Mr. Simon took advantage of the price appreciation of the art by donating it to his museum and then took a hefty tax write off. Millionaires don't need to buy expensive cars even though they can afford it. They know they are wealthy and don't care to impress anyone else because they don't have to; they have more than a million dollars and so can you.

⌒

FOR OVER 35 YEARS, MERI ANNE has managed investments for an expanded client base including Norton Simon and the Federal Reserve Pension Fund. She is a member of the CFA Institute, the Los Angeles Society of Financial Analysts, a past President of the Los Angeles Association of Investment Women, and a lifetime member of the Network for Empowering Women Entrepreneurs. She is Chairman, CFO, and Co-founder of Odyssey Advisors where she manages investments for high net-worth individuals, families, and institutions. You can reach her direct at 310-568-4700 or visit online at www.OdysseyAdvisors.com.

CHAPTER 15

De-Clutter, De-Stress & Design Your Office Space

DEE E. BEHRMAN

CLUTTER is defined as:

- (*noun*) Crowded confusion
- (*noun*) A heap or assemblage of things lying in confusion, litter
- (*verb*) To fill with scattered things that impede movement or reduce efficiency
- (*verb*) To crowd together in disorder
- (*verb*) To jumble, to fill with confusion.

For many years, I have witnessed and experienced the struggle and frustration most of us have as a result of:

1. Office environments not designed to optimize productivity, efficiency or personal effectiveness.
2. Poor infrastructures regarding paper and filing systems—both electronic and hard copy documents.
3. Inability to manage time in terms of all that needs to be accomplished.
4. Deficient follow-up systems.

Positive transformations will occur by creating and implementing custom systems and methods to alleviate the burden of clutter and information overwhelm.

Why are we inundated with clutter and paper? Both the good and bad news is we have more choices, conveniences and information. Their impact on our lives has created stressful and unmanageable working conditions.

Recently, I ran to the store to get my usual crackers, cheese and wine for an out of town guest. The next thing I knew, I was standing in front of the crackers in a daze. I must have been there for about 30 seconds before I snapped out of my trance long enough to learn my crackers now come in six different variations—low sodium, extra large, all wheat. . . !

While this is just a case of **more** cracker choices, this kind of expansion is happening in *every* facet of our lives.

Because we have so many choices, it is becoming increasingly difficult to make decisions.

The paradox is that conveniences are adding to our overwhelm and clutter. Think about it. . . each time a product purchase is made there are many processes.

Before purchasing a product, you need to research its useful-ness and cost-effectiveness. After the purchase, you need to learn how to use the product, store the warranty and contact informa-tion for the product, possibly insure/warranty the product, main-tain the product, know how to use the product properly and who to call when the product is not working. Yet another decision is whether to replace the product when a newer, faster and better version has been introduced.

Years ago, we'd buy something (without half the hassles of research because there weren't as many choices), and we would own it for many years—no problem. In fact, there were electronic and fix-it shops we could take our appliances and equipment to if they broke down. Nowadays, everything from an answering machine to an expensive piece of computer equipment is a throw-away item if we don't buy the extended warranty. It's mind-bog-gling. We have been given so much more to think about and be responsible for!

People are starting to realize their stuff, their papers, and their conveniences are not producing the quality of life they had antici-pated and imagined.

Recently, a conference was held at UCLA where attendees learned about how to create a simpler and more satisfying life. The conference was called "Mental Health and Simple Living—Countering the Compulsion to Consume."

Although our modern world has dramatically improved our material lives, stress levels have become increasingly high and have raised major concerns for mental health professionals.

Contrary to the myth of the Paperless Society, the Computer Age has produced a glut of paper. Office paper is the fastest grow-ing segment of this challenge. People are printing out everything they see—websites, email, etc. Hewlett Packard estimates that laser printers spewed out 1.2 trillion sheets of paper in 2003, and there's a projected increase of 50% within the next 5 years. Fax machines, photocopiers and other devices add greatly to that number.

Most of us are so inundated that we are unable to think clearly or live *mindfully*. The inability to think clearly produces one or more of the following reactions:

a. *Paralysis*—where thinking is clouded and the decision-making process is extremely difficult, if not impossible. If it is impossi-ble to make a decision, the situation progresses to a condition called "procrastination."

b. *Procrastination*—whereby things keep getting put off, creating a downward cycle of not wanting to deal with anything because the tasks have become too daunting.

c. *Trance state*—not being in the present moment, resulting in not remembering things such as information, procedures, systems and prioritization of tasks. This happens when your mind becomes so filled with information from your body and environment that your subconscious mind takes over. This trance state has also been referred to as automatism, automaticity, automatic pilot and highway hypnosis.

d. *Confusion* and vagueness resulting in the inability to create a plan of action, a system or prioritization of work to be done.

The more choices we have and the more we have to think about, the greater the probability we may temporarily become paralyzed, procrastinate, go into a trance state and/or become confused.

These things can become especially bothersome if we are in a rush to complete a task under an imminent deadline.

A common example of this is losing our keys. Most of us have had the experience of putting our keys down, assuming we put them in an easy location to remember. Our actions are so automatic, we are actually thinking of something else as we put down the keys, and we don't consciously note where we put them. Then in a rush to leave, we need the keys, but we do not remember where they are. This stress creates panic, frustration and the inability to think clearly.

Now that we can see and understand what has happened, what can we do about it? Our personal effectiveness depends on our *relationship* with everything in our office environment including the furniture, information systems and equipment. How conveniently everything is arranged in our work environment greatly affects our productivity and satisfaction in completing the myriad of tasks we are required to perform.

DESIGN OF THE OFFICE ENVIRONMENT FALLS INTO
THE FOLLOWING CATEGORIES

- *Office Furniture and Equipment Configuration*
  Office furniture and equipment should be placed so everything is convenient to the user. Items used most often should be within easy reach.
- *Office Environment—Aesthetics*
  Colors, art, flowers and plants are important components of the office environment.
- *Information Management—Hard Copy and Electronic*
  Simple, straightforward processes for handling information are critical. Recording all of the systems and procedures is very important. Use notebooks and sign ins. Have them handy. Do your best to be accountable and responsible for each procedure.
- *Communication with Team Members*
  Team members must have clear and effective communication with one another. Breakdowns are symptoms of regular miscommunication. It is important to remember everyone has a different frame of reference. Understandings and agreements need to be confirmed so that everyone is clear about the objectives. Back it up with email or documentation.
- *Time Management Systems*
  Calendar Systems are to be set up for timely follow-up, so there is no confusion about time frames and other date-related deadlines.
- *Emergency Procedures*
  Emergency procedures are to be delineated for all office workers, including home-based business workers.

Anything done to simplify and upgrade systems, as well as to reduce confusion, will create an atmosphere for more productive, effective and successful completion of tasks.

When people are able to work in a convenient and user-friendly environment, productivity naturally increases; this creates the ability to work smarter, not harder.

⌐‿‿⌐

DEE comes with 20 years of experience in creating highly functional and aesthetically refreshing office environments. She has been featured in the LA Times, Torrance Daily Breeze, Culver City News, Culver City People and WIPI (Women In Photography International) She received Rubbermaid's CHOISE (Center for Home Organization and Interior Space Efficiency) Award. Dee is the Creator of the breakthrough 7-Point Paper Management System, a process of paper flow for any office professional guaranteed to work! 310.216.6607 www.organizeyourspace.com | clutterguru@organizeyourspace.com.

CHAPTER 16

Big Business Success

It's Closer Than You Think

KIM CASTLE

EVER FIND YOURSELF going great distances for something you want and when you find it, you realize it was in your backyard all along? It's the same with succeeding in an entrepreneurial business. Often small business owners put the power of building their business in their customers, when that's what often drives them to fail. Don't misunderstand. Customers are paramount, but big business success *starts* with defining how 'big' you really want your business to be. The only person in charge of that is. . . you.

The question I hear most while speaking on branding is, "Am I too small to develop my business as a brand?" That's like asking me, "Is my business too small to make money?" Is your business too small to make money? I should hope not. Surely there are more fun things you could do—like hanging out on the beaches of Hawaii.

At a recent luncheon, I was seated next to an attorney whose sole practice focuses on elder abuse. He asked me in rapid succession (in a manner illustrating he'd be great in court):

"Isn't branding for businesses that make a lot of stuff?"
"Doesn't branding only apply if you want to sell a lot of stuff?"
"Isn't branding pointless for my kind of business?"

Smiling, I fired back, "Yes, yes, and. . . no."

Yes, branding is most often associated with businesses that make a lot of stuff. *Yes*, branding is advantageous if you want to sell a lot of stuff. *No*, branding is not pointless because every business makes something including valuable services and wants to sell it—hopefully a lot of it. Branding is about making your product or service known to as many potential customers as possible on a consistent basis by the most effective use of your time and money. Branding is about repeat business; it is about effortless referrals. Wouldn't that be a benefit to ANY business, especially yours? The really cool thing. . . about branding is it really *starts* with a mindset . . . yours!

You don't have to be Disney or Coke to be a brand; small business can have brand power, too. In fact, to stand out from all the other entrepreneurs just like you—it's essential! The only thing you need is the right mindset to unleash it. It's your mindset that sets your entire business in motion—whether you acknowledge it or not.

Your mindset determines your behavior and outlook, which in turn delivers your outcome—in this case—clear, holistic and instant communication of your business. A brand mindset ensures bigger success because you begin with a bigger end in mind. And if you throw passion into the mix, you'll be cooking with limitless fuel.

The thing that stops most small business owners from stepping into a brand mindset is—fear. Fear that their business isn't worthy of that much effort. Fear they don't have the money to make it?

Fear that if they do make it, nobody will buy it? Fear their spouse or partner will think they've gone crazy? Or, even fear that friends and colleagues will think they're egotistical? Fear is something your mind puts in your way to protect you. Your brain is just doing its job by instilling fear and trepidation over something new. Your brain is making itself worthy to you.

The first step to diminishing fear is to simply thank your mind for doing its job and move beyond it. It's time to get out of your own way. It's as easy as taking your hands down from in front of your face. Think about the roadblocks you may have set up for yourself. Often these roadblocks keep you—safe. Safe never made anybody financially successful. The roadblocks keep you mired in the emotional busywork of getting through them so that you never really have to accomplish what you really want. Some people get so good at overcoming these "obstacles," they forget what they started out to do. To develop a brand mindset, you need to be aware of the roadblocks you have put in the way, learn how to walk around them, and eventually break free of creating them ever again.

You're taking a great first step by starting right here. You are expanding your knowledge, opening your awareness and adopting a new mindset. Add to this mindset the belief you can manifest all you need, when you need it, and you will move boldly towards creating your big business success.

With vision in focus, passion in place, and fear out of the way, even if momentarily, you can avoid a common fallacy business owners have when starting to brand their business. MISCONCEPTION #1: You need a logo or a website. . . first. This couldn't be farther from the truth. Not that these tools aren't important. They are very important and necessary! The issue is believing they come first. It's understandable. Most potential clients see these things first. They are external forms of communication.

Think of building your brand as if you were making a fantastic ice cream sundae. Your logo is the juicy cherry on top, your website is the creamy whipped cream, your brochure and leave-behinds are jimmies and nuts. So what's missing? That's right—the ice cream! What kind of ice cream is your business? The choices are as diverse and as individual as you.

Begin from the inside when developing your business or product as a brand, then and only then, will you successfully communicate it outwardly to your potential clients with an amazing logo, website and other exciting marketing tools. If you don't go from the inside out, your clients won't "feel" your value. You can overcome them with shear will or force, but it won't last. Your business won't effortlessly build exponentially. Additionally, as a brand, you'll always have an easier time of knowing what serves your business and customers and what does not.

"This all sounds good," you say, "but how do I start internally?"

In three simple steps:
- First, *set aside the need to have a new logo or web site* or any other external communication tools. If you currently have one you are using, continue to use it through your brand development stage. Any art created during this stage is akin to building multi-story building of concrete walls on sand without a foundation.
- Second, *block out the need to reach out to your customer,* just during this developmental stage. Trying to keep both your brand and marketing to your customer on equal footing will create the Swiss Cheese Syndrome: a brand filled with holes.
- Third, *focus internally on what your business is all about*—what you are truly bringing the world through your product or service. You must determine your business' internal reason to be in existence.

Once these three things are accomplished, then and only then, should you begin to develop the tools for communicating your business—to yourself, next to your team, and finally to the world. The time you take internally will result in exponential growth when you take it out in all its glory.

So you see, a brand mindset is not only for the Cokes and Disneys of the world. It's for you! So, if you have a big vision of your business, you are passionate about it, it brings value to people, and you envision a big financial reward from it then. . . develop your business as a brand.

Your big business success is in your own backyard—waiting for you to declare it. Why wait? Your business and the world are waiting with their hearts (and their wallets) open.

With a background in global advertising, KIM CASTLE has helped hundreds of small business owners grow their business to new heights of success. The co-author of **Why BrandU Big Business Success No Matter Your Size** *and the* **BrandU Bible**, *the only step-by-step branding workbook, Castle is also the illuminating presenter of the popular BrandU? workshops where she motivates, entertains and raises the bar on business communication like no other! Reach her at kim@whybrandu.com or www.whybrandu.com.*

CHAPTER 17

I Had A Good Feeling About You

LISA CHERNEY

"WHY WOULD YOU GO TO WORK for someone else when you can work for yourself?" I looked to my right to see where this voice was coming from. There was no one there. I was stuck in traffic on the freeway, coming from work on a Friday afternoon having just been laid off, and I was terrified! My husband had quit his job as a chemical engineer three months ago to follow his dream of attending chiropractic college. This disembodied voice was obviously out of its mind!

I was going to be the sole support of our family for the next four years; I had to find a job! And fast! However, I soon realized the voice was, in fact, within my own mind. Until that moment, I had never, ever, thought of starting my own company. I didn't realize until that very moment I had a dream, too! Thoughts of FREEDOM danced in my head, right along with fearful images of losing our house. But could I possibly own my own business? Was there any way? The voice persisted and that weekend was an emotional roller coaster ride.

It is now five years later, and not only did we keep our house, but I have a thriving business—Conscious Marketing™—and my husband has a flourishing chiropractic practice and is happier then he's ever been. When I worry about taking risks and following my intuition, I always look back on the day I heard that voice. At the time, it said something completely illogical, but what I felt in my body was pure elation! Now I know after years of practice and "connecting to my inner voice" that what my mind/body told me has given me a thriving business full of joy. In addition, it has surrounded me with talented, soulful people who contribute to my life and spiritual growth

Conscious Marketing is my own unique, from-the-inside-out marketing approach, where I assist small and medium-sized business owners and executives in balancing their heads and their hearts through workshops and one-on-one sessions using guided imagery, spontaneous discussion and other heart-based techniques. My role as a coach and consultant is to show my clients that when they trust their inner voice, or intuition, their feelings act as an internal compass.

The results are passion-filled marketing materials, great team leadership, uplifted management styles and many more benefits as each person clears away all the static. Everything grows out of each client's vision of the true value of his or her business and what one has to share with the world. It is a most remarkable journey I take with people I work with; one that thrills and astounds me as well as each of them! Following gut level instincts ensures that you find joy in your work. When you reach this level of satisfaction, success is nearly guaranteed!

Your intuition is handy for all kinds of decisions, from everyday issues like setting prices and deciding which clients to work with, to larger concepts like the content of your marketing material and which vendors or suppliers to hire.

For example, I was at a networking event recently and during the brief, initial introductions, I overheard a woman talking about how she "helps companies integrate business systems." I wasn't clear on exactly what that meant, but there was something that attracted me to her. I had to leave early, but before I slipped out, I quietly asked for her card. It was my intuition telling me to call her. My logic was saying, "You don't even know her! No one has recommended her! What if she is incompetent?" I listened to the fear voice (I also call this ego) for a while because, at times, it's pretty loud.

Her card sat on my desk for a few days, but then I put my fear/ego aside. I literally asked it to take a seat and called her. Guess what? My intuition was right on! It's a year later, and this woman has been an absolute lifesaver! She has handled a complicated tax issue, upgraded my financial software, integrated all my databases and is always keeping an eye on the future of my business.

I received all of these benefits from following my instincts. Recently she asked me why I initially called her, and all I could say was, "I had a good feeling about you!"

Here are a few questions to ask yourself when you have a decision to make and aren't sure if you are ignoring your intuition:

1. Does it feel like I'm going against logic? (Don't be afraid if it doesn't seem to make sense initially.)
2. If money weren't an object, what would I do? (Act as if you were a millionaire.)
3. Is my fear voice (or ego) clouding my decision? (Read on for "affirmations.")
4. Am I afraid of what people (or a particular person) might think? (Whose name is on your business card?)
5. Is my head saying one thing, but my body another? (i.e. Your head says, "Are you crazy?" but are you feeling excitement in your body?)

Another way to follow your inner guidance is to pay attention to external signs. For instance, as my personal spiritual journey progressed, I began to acknowledge signs and tools like affirmations and setting intentions, and I found myself using prayer in my business.

This more fully connected me to my intuition and to a Higher Power (which you may also wish to call "the Universe" or "God"). As I opened myself to affirmations, intentions and prayer more and more, I began to see more signs. Sometimes they looked like coincidences, while at other times, they appeared as advice or suggestions from a friend.

A good example of a sign I noticed and acted upon occurred last month. I was contemplating whether or not to attend a networking event early the next morning. A guy I had met earlier asked me if I was planning to attend the meeting the following morning, and I told him I wasn't sure yet. (You see, by now I'm used to waiting for signs/my intuition to guide me, and I hadn't had any stirrings.)

He strongly suggested I go, saying the speaker was going to be quite outstanding. Early the next morning I remembered his enthusiasm and, of course, I decided to go. I wound up making a great connection with the speaker, who asked me to participate in a "virtual university" he is creating for entrepreneurs; it's going to be a wonderful opportunity to share the Conscious Marketing message. All this occurred because I followed the signs!

When you begin to listen to your inner guidance system, answers will come to you in many forms. Answers to your questions seem to be there when you need them, especially if you stay positive by affirming yourself and your business.

Here's an example of an affirmation I use regularly in my business: "Wherever I go, I connect with the perfect people to support my business." This always ensures I meet or sit next to just the right person at networking meetings.

Be sure to use positive, present tense language when making affirmations. The best time to create affirmations is when the "fear voice" is the loudest in your head. Take the negative thought and turn it into a positive affirmation that articulates what you want.

Instead of focusing on what you don't want, change it immediately from, "I can't make money doing this," to "All clients I attract willingly pay my fees." (This is one of my favorites.) When affirmation meets your intuition and you follow the signs, you are sure to walk your divine path.

Many people call on the Universe in their personal lives, but often they don't use its power in their businesses. The way I see it, your business is an extension of your service on this planet. Therefore, when you are working, you should also be divinely inspired. It's time to let your inner voice guide you in all that you do.

Take time to listen to the feelings in your body; your inner guidance will transport you to a new level that you can trust as you learn this remarkable language of self. It takes courage to live an authentic life and make decisions based on your intuition. However, when you follow your heart, everyone around you benefits. People will sit next to you and say, "I had a good feeling about you!"

LISA CHERNEY is a Marketing Coach & Business Consultant and President of Conscious Marketing, founded in 1999. Lisa held marketing and training positions at Fortune 500 companies like AT&T and Lipton for 15 years. She was also an Account Executive at top advertising agencies with clients like Nissan and Land O'Lakes. A dynamic speaker, Lisa has spoken to thousands of business owners to help "Knock 'Em Conscious" and market their business from the "inside out." Visit www.ConsciousMarketing.com or call 1-888-771-0156.

CHAPTER 18

Speak Your Business In 30 Seconds Or Less™

ANN CONVERY

Hi! How are you? What do you do?

I'VE JUST MET YOU. In eight seconds, I've secretly decided your success level, your education, your income, your status, and six other intangibles. I'm a typical American, so I have about a nine-second attention span—that's the same as a goldfish. I don't care what you do, really. I'm a nice person, but I don't have time. I'm too busy caring about all the things that are screaming for attention in my head—my kids, my husband, and my job. But I'm polite.

Your mission, should you decide to accept it, is to hook my interest and snap it to attention on you and your service. You have 30 seconds. How will you do it?

A 30-second message is also called a verbal business card. You use your verbal business card 22 more times than your paper card. How much blood, sweat and tears went into designing that paper card? How about your verbal card, which has an infinitely greater selling power?

1. "I'm a mortgage broker. I help people find their dream homes." —Sue
2. "I teach people five secrets of equity and finance, so they can leverage other people's money and hang on to more of their own." —Sue after "30-Second" Training

The first message is an educational message. Trouble is, if you're not looking for a dream home, you don't need Sue. Glazed eyeballs. You've mentally checked out.

The second statement is a marketing message—its purpose is to hook interest, grab focus, and create urgency to know more about *you, now.* Sue's marketplace is now much larger. It includes everyone who's interested in money, an emotional hot button.

Sue is also perceived as an expert, since she teaches. Verbs are the most powerful engines in the English language. If you say, "I am an attorney" and I don't need one, I mentally check out. But if you can teach, create, design, repackage, or reveal—then maybe you can fulfill one of my needs. I'll keep listening.

Sue has a number of secrets, and numbers are magic. They create urgency. People often tell me that prospective clients remember the numbers long after the message. Why are numbers so powerful? Because we measure our lives by them. What's your age? Weight? Income? SAT score? If Sue has five secrets you don't have, she has a kind of power—there's an irresistible urge to ask, "What are they?!" That's why the media loves numbers: The Top Ten Best-Dressed List. Eight Rules for a Great Marriage. Numbers are like peanuts, you can't eat just one.

In the second message Sue directly addresses a basic need—hanging on to your money. A dream home is fabulous—someday. Your money is something you can emotionally connect with right now. Sue's referrals tripled after she began using message No. 2.

What are you *really* selling? Can you touch a need that keeps your prospects up at night? More money, better relationships and better health are three of the most basic needs we have. What need are you fulfilling for your clients? A bigger client base, healthier bottom line, more personal time? That's what you want your prospects to feel on an emotional level—not what you do, but what you can do *for them*.

So you've given your marketing message and they ask for more. Now what?

THE SECOND LINER

The secret to the second-liner is to keep hooking your listeners. Don't give away the store. When I worked with Sue, the mortgage broker, we came up with ten second-liners. For example, "I can take you from a B- to an A listing in a year and a half." Create a one-sentence success story. Give a range of your ability. Use testimonials. Raise the bar. For example, a PR firm can say, "Yes, we just had a client in *Time*, but we found that a profile in *The Wall Street Journal* brought more response."

Now that you've developed your message, how do you put it into a megaphone? Take it to the media.

THE MEDIA

I've spent 14 years in PR and media training, preparing clients for *CNN, 60 Minutes, The Today Show, Good Morning America, The New York Times, The Wall Street Journal*, and many other outlets. This was where I learned to absorb 30 years of a client's professional experience and put it into two sound bites that would be remembered after the news was over. When I began hearing, "I wish I'd had this training before I went into court," or "I wish I'd spoken to you before I pitched the VC's," I realized how powerful the media pitch can be for business professionals.

The media is not interested in you, your product or your service. The media is hungry for terrific stories. You are as valuable to them as your stories. Your clients, your successes, problems you've solved, trends you've discovered—these are your stories. Tie your service to a trend, holiday, or controversy. Debunk a myth. Ask provocative questions. Answer the media's "So What?" factor. Is your pitch relevant to Americans right now? What happens if I don't use your product or service? Disaster? How big? Tell me more.

Target your media audience. Scan the news. Call the local TV news before 9 a.m. and tell them briefly that you are an expert on a story that broke in this morning's paper. Read the magazines and newspapers and get to know the editors so you can mention their articles when you pitch (a huge plus). Write a press release. Give yourself the sharpest hook you can find for a headline. Stumped? Go to the supermarket and read the headlines: Three Mistakes Smart Women Make with Money. Five Signs You're in a Work Slump. In the first paragraph, state the problem, why it's urgent right now, how it's affecting singles, marrieds, kids, babies, moms, dads, teachers, whoever, and how your profession can solve it. Then create eight to ten bullet points on how you can address the topic— these are story angles. Make your bio one paragraph. Put your name and contact information at the bottom. Call to find out if the editor or producer likes email, fax, or snail.

When following up with editors by phone ask, "Is this a good time for me to call?" If no, ask when you can call again. When pitching, you have 20-30 seconds to make it interesting to the editor, who has to make it interesting to her editor. Tell her a great, heart-breaking, little known, fascinating story with national implications in 20 seconds. Give her five different angles. Ask her what she's working on. Could you be a resource for her?

Can you get on *Oprah*? You can try. Study the show and the story hooks. Target the producer you will pitch. Remember you are only a part of a bigger story. Is there a huge hidden problem you see happening in America? Do you have case studies? Statistics? Clients who will go on? Could you do a makeover? Carefully cast your entire segment. Then mail your pitch to the producer you've chosen.

You now have three ways to create buzz for your business. Develop your 30-second pitch. Create second liners until you have 75% of your listeners saying, "Really? Tell me more!" Contact the media. Start with just one media outlet until you establish a relationship, and become a media resource one story at a time.

ANN CONVERY, M.A., is a high-performance communication coach who has worked with former Mayor Richard Riordan, entrepreneurs and corporate professionals for over 15 years. Ann has coached hundreds of clients to build national reputations and to increase their sales, referrals, and word-of-mouth. She has been interviewed in Elle, Cosmopolitan, ABC-TV, Maxim, Fitness, Woman's Day, Entrepreneur and other media. Harper Collins will publish her second book in 2005. For a mini-review, contact: 323-644-7955 annc@annconvery.com

CHAPTER 19

How To Stay In Your Pajamas All Day. . . And Still Run A Business

ELISA GOODMAN

I'D NEVER THOUGHT OF MYSELF as an "artist" when I first started making greeting cards. I didn't go to art school but have always been creative. If I have to read a "how-to" textbook, then I'd rather forget it. My first notion of starting my own business began during my husband's mid-life crisis when he went from being an attorney to a librarian! It was illuminating to say the least, especially when he mentioned a possible move to another state! As a casting director in Los Angeles for 18 years, I was comfortable living in L.A. near my family & friends and definitely did not want to move.

After my father passed away, my mom's Feng-Shui cleaning returned my childhood stamp collection to me and I decided to use my stamps in my card designs. In creating my first designs, I realized if I got this company off the ground, I could make cards ANY-WHERE in the world, at HOME and even in my PAJAMAS! If I needed to see clients or expand my home base, I could exhibit at Trade Shows. My custom-collage card idea was to create greeting cards for under $8.00 each and market them to "hard-to-buy-for" people. Because of the extensive nature of topics on stamps, I also marketed the cards for current Museum Exhibitions and specialty gift shops around the country.

Easily bored, the short-term nature of casting and designing solved my restlessness. I love that on any given day I might be using Dogs, Modigliani, Baseball or Audrey Hepburn! After a series of "home parties," my friend Kitty Swink walked me into PERGOLINA in Toluca Lake, and this became my first professional sale. One store became five, and soon I was up to 100. I was also fortunate that Cim Castellon, the buyer at The Los Angeles County Museum of Art, took my initial call and agreed to meet with me without sending samples first.

STARTING MY DAY IN MY PAJAMAS

At 7am I make my latte and get to work. The most exciting aspect of the morning is unveiling the 50-75 new cards I made the night before which I now have available to sell! Next to a really big sale, that is invigorating!

The kind of day it is—paperwork, ordering, prepping, setting up or going on appointments (where I would actually have to get dressed and leave the house before 5 p.m.), determines my mood. On appointment days, I clean the house and do anything that makes me feel organized. Around 4 p.m. I usually get out of my pajamas, take a shower and run errands.

MOTIVATING TIPS

It is hard to be the buggy, horse, driver and WHIP! If it is a day to make phone calls and you encounter (3-5) resistance calls, consider this might not be the right day to continue with the calls. When it is not going your way, it takes extra energy to continue. LEAVE THE HOUSE and go to Yoga or take a walk. It's a way to do something nice for yourself and clear your mind. When I don't feel productive it feels like a wasted day. When I tell my husband it's "hard" and money is tight—he tells me that if I think it's supposed to be easy then I should throw everything out and get a real job! I can't even imagine that now.

BEST ADVICE

Say "YES" to everything.

Don't "COMPARE" and "DESPAIR" yourself with others. It's debilitating and causes non-action & depression.

Set money goals for the week or the number of stores you want appointments with. Being realistic works better for me. If I "overestimate" and don't complete my goal, I feel like I've failed so I'd rather have smaller goals and go beyond them if I can.

I'm good at selling and don't believe in "slick marketing or hard sales". If they want it, great. If not, it wasn't right for them *FOR WHATEVER REASON*. They can love my cards and still not buy. I've actually gotten referrals to other stores from buyers! I don't need to be everywhere—just in the *RIGHT* stores for my product.

Don't cancel appointments unless absolutely necessary. IT IS VERY HARD TO GET BACK IN THE DOOR! Call to confirm the day before. I've pushed myself to go in the rain, if I'm sick, etc. It's all about showing up—FOR YOURSELF!

HANDY TIPS

Investigate all leads. Check out the store ambiance and merchandise before you call the owner or send samples. If you want your samples back, enclose a SASE envelope. When your friends go out of town, ask them to look for stores and pick up a business card with the buyer's info for you.

I always go into the store with samples in my bag just in case I "happen" to run into the owner/buyer who inquires why I'm looking around. Know your market and price points, and don't be afraid to ask what you think they are worth. Don't undersell yourself—it's too hard to raise your prices later. They will always make things cheaper somewhere else. But what they are ultimately buying is *YOU* and your *UNIQUENESS*.

Have your mother pimp for you. (That's what I do). She gives my cards as gifts (instead of candy) when she's invited to dinner. She goes into my stores to see what my competition is, how many cards they have left, AND, she's steered customers to my cards without revealing who she is! She's available . . . Call her!

For new accounts, call or e-mail to see how the product is doing. Many customers trust my taste even though they haven't seen what they have ordered ahead of time. You can troubleshoot a problem if the product isn't moving or offer to exchange it the next time you visit them. You want to be able to get in the door a second time.

KARMA TIPS

My strength is connecting people. I recommend other card artists to my customers if I think they would be an asset to them. Obviously, their cards are different than mine. Good, classy hand-made cards help stores gain a reputation for innovative merchandise.

Reciprocate when you can, and buy from your stores since it helps to even out the relationship—this way they don't feel you're always "selling" something. Give holiday gifts. It's always good for them to *Thank You* the next time you call.

KEEPING IT TOGETHER

Putting off stuff because it feels icky? Try this: Don't say "deal with"— say "I need to complete this" instead. "Deal with" implies it will take a long time; there will be obstacles, etc. "Complete this" means the problem/solution is already in the works, needing a couple of items before it goes away. Pick (5) things you have been putting off and do those today. Many times I can even do more if the day is going well.

I would prefer to be making cards to anything else. However, if I'm behind, I REWARD myself with designing when I'm finished with the hard stuff. Resistance for me is anything that requires reading long stretches of legal documents, asking for money from clients who have not paid on time, research, math-related issues and delegating.

SPENDING MONEY

I'm conservative because cash flow is usually tight. If clients don't pay on time, it becomes tricky. Because of this, I now take credit cards. I really wanted to make sure I still loved making cards and decided I would grow my business slowly. I push myself to the max every day to see what my productivity rate is so I know at what point I'll need to hire someone to help me.

Other costs to consider include: phone, permits (you need separate ones for wholesale and retail), legal fees for trademark and copyright issues, advertising, printing, supplies, bank fees, etc.

My satisfaction abounds when people who have received my cards find me, find my website or hear about me. The power of the world finding you is awesome!

In March, I got a call from a girl who said my cards inspired her to open a store in her hometown as they only carried Hallmark where she lived. Her father encouraged her to follow her passion for greeting cards and "GO FOR IT". I always feel it will work out in the end. And if it's right, it never feels like work! It feels like staying in your pajamas until 5pm and enjoying life!

ELISA GOODMAN has been a casting director for 18 years and has co-taught marketing seminars for actors at UCLA. Her husband's mid-life crisis set a new path in motion for her to find another career. Her custom-collage greeting card company, curmudgeon cards (The Art of Finding the "Perfect" Card) was born three years ago. Her unique art cards have been featured in museum and specialty gift shops around the country. (877) 395-2044 (Toll-Free) or (310) 475-7994 (from Los Angeles) curmudgeoncards@earthlink.net www.curmudgeoncards.com

CHAPTER 20

Self-Identity = Business Success

Discovering The Real You

MABEL KATZ

THE MOST IMPORTANT QUESTION you can ever ask yourself is "Who Am I?" Sadly, some of us get so busy "doing life," making money, creating families, running businesses, starting new careers—that we never really stop to figure out who we really are.

Knowing yourself is realizing you were created as a unique being, and there is something special you can do better than anybody else. Once you figure out what it is, by discovering the true YOU, everything else will fall into place. It's the secret to your success and happiness, business-wise and everything-else-wise.

Until I learned this, I was weighed down by trying to be perfect and do what others expected of me. I believed my happiness was in the material things, and I paid little attention to what my heart really wanted. I only believed in those things I could see or touch. Then one day, when my son yelled at me in the same angry voice I'd been using for years with him. I had a sudden awakening; it was time to work on myself.

My path to self-discovery led me to the principles of the ancient Hawaiian art of Ho'oponopono, which I'm sharing with you here. It saved my life! I started my own business after separating from 20 plus years of marriage. I got out of my own way and began to trust my inner wisdom, letting the part of me that knows best guide me. I let go of opinions and judgments of others, and myself and now, I have more than I ever would have imagined in every area of my life.

Growing up we are either told to be perfect or we are not good enough. It's human nature to go through life unconsciously replaying those "old tapes" in our heads. The day I realized I could just be myself, a big weight lifted off my shoulders. Let me be the first to tell you if you don't already know: You are okay just the way you are.

What other people think of you is not important; what's important is what you think of yourself. You need to learn to put yourself first. The truth is, if something doesn't work for you, it will not be good for anybody. Loving and accepting yourself has nothing to do with ego. If you do not love yourself, you cannot love anybody else. You cheat them—and yourself.

There are a few simple principles and steps to help you look at your life differently and develop a new "true" self image, which will in turn, translate into the success you are seeking.

TAKING 100% RESPONSIBILITY

Take 100% responsibility for whatever is going on in your life. Once you realize it is just your tapes playing, you can choose to stop them. They are like programs in the computer of your mind. If they weren't installed there, they wouldn't play. When a situation comes up, and you know it's just the tapes playing, (you'll learn to recognize them easier as you go along) use the "delete key" in the keyboard of your mind and erase the thought that created or attracted the situation. I know what you're thinking: How do I know which thought created it? Don't worry; there is a part of you that knows. You just need to give permission.

Once we take 100% responsibility, we discover we have two choices. We are free to replay the old tapes, or come from a deeper place inside, which I call inner wisdom or "inspiration." Instead of having to be "right," blame or judge, we can choose in any given moment to let go and experience who we really are; we will have the power to change our lives without depending on anybody or anything.

LETTING GO

Letting go can correct a multitude of errors. One of the best ways is to be thankful for everything that comes to you, even when it's hard to see it as a blessing. When you have a thankful attitude, doors will open and opportunities will abound! They will seemingly come from nowhere! You can simply repeat in your mind: thank you, thank you, thank you. Saying thank you is a way of letting go, a way of not engaging, not judging, not having opinions. It's a way of daily living and breathing. As soon as you have opinions of right or wrong, you're stuck. It's those old tapes playing again. You can stop them and delete them by saying " thank you."

Whenever the old tapes come up, better yet before they start playing, say "thank you" to yourself. What you are doing is taking 100% responsibility and saying, "I'm sorry, please forgive me for whatever is in me that has created or attracted this into my life. Thank you for showing me this negative thought pattern so I can erase it."

Another secret for letting go is having no expectations. You will be amazed at what God has in store for you when you release your expectations. Many times we are unaware of the outcome already planned in our minds. Be aware to not be aware! Know you are powerful beyond your wildest dreams and capable of attracting everything that is right for you—even if it doesn't seem to fit the "perfect" picture. Most of all, realize that every "no" is usually for a good reason, even if you can't see it at the time. It means something better and greater is coming your way. Every "no" is an opportunity to take responsibility and be grateful.

BRINGING YOUR "TRUE SELF" TO BUSINESS.

Why is bringing your "true self" important when it comes to making money, or having a successful business? Wouldn't you like to be always in the perfect place at the right time? Wouldn't you like to attract the right people to work in your business? Attract the best customers? Manifest money effortlessly?

Knowing who you are, your own God-given talents and gifts you were born with, not the ones you have acquired or were told you were "supposed" to have, is a surefire way to attract success in all you do. Simply think about something you would do because you feel so good doing it that you would do it even if you weren't paid to do it—and you will discover your talents fit the same picture. This is a true alignment with your soul purpose.

People can tell when you love what you're doing. Business just comes to you. Money shows up in your life. You are in the right place at the right time. You are willing to feel the fear and do it anyway—because you trust yourself!

LETTING IT WORK FOR YOU

Have you ever noticed when you are happy, (sometimes for no apparent reason) good things just happen to you? You receive a phone call you didn't expect? You felt inspired to go to a party where you met one of your best customers? Money somebody owed you for a long time suddenly comes in the mail? Why do you think this happens? Maybe you got out of your own way! Everything in your life is a blessing, even if it doesn't look like it.

Remember, your intellect does not know what is right and perfect for you. Allow the universe to surprise you. Your dreams can come true when you least expect it. "Everything" is up to you. The sky is the limit. It's just you and your thoughts—which you have the power to change at every moment of every day.

MABEL KATZ is the author of "The Easiest Way." Solve your problems and take the road to love, happiness, wealth and the life of your dreams. Her passion is sharing the power people have to change their lives. She hosts a radio program called "Despertar" (Awakening) and travels around the world "waking people up" with her lectures and seminars. Mabel is president of Your Business, Inc., where as an accountant she helps others create successful businesses. You can contact Mabel by visiting www.businessbyyou.com and www.mabelkatz.com

CHAPTER 21

Prosperity & Harmony
In The Workplace

Using Feng Shui And Intentional Design Principles

MADELEINE LaFONTAINE

IS YOUR OFFICE DRESSED FOR SUCCESS, or designed for struggle, disappointment, and failure? Does it inspire you? Have you reached your goals or fulfilled your dreams in your current workplace? The quality of your life can be dramatically influenced, positively or negatively, by the qualities of your living and working environments. A beautiful functional space can give you the inspiration, peace, and freedom to live your optimal life.

I am passionate about Feng Shui. Eight years ago I tried it out when my life seemed hectic and unbalanced raising my triplets, who were then three years old. Using the ancient common sense principles of Feng Shui under the guidance of master Rich Welt, my days flowed more easily, even though my daily schedule remained the same.

I was ecstatic. A perfect next step in my development as an interior designer, Rich began to train me extensively. Since then, I have applied these practices to my design business with much success.

In this chapter, I would like to share some key principles of Feng Shui and provide a sprinkle of ideas on how to change the set-up and energy of your environment to create prosperity, improve your relationships, and achieve a more balanced life. By combining Feng Shui (the ancient science of moving energy, or "chi," to attract whatever you want) with my interior design experience and practice, coupled with what I learned as a coach, I've created many "magical" things for my family, friends, clients and myself. There's no reason why you can't achieve the same results yourself. Here's my basic approach:

STEP ONE: IDENTIFY YOUR GOALS
(THIS WOULD BE HOMEWORK):

FIRST, ASK YOURSELF:

"What are my career goals?" "What are my personal goals?" Write them down.

THEN, ASK YOURSELF:

"In what areas am I experiencing success?" "In what areas am I falling short?" "What are the chronic complaints I have about my life or my work?"

Take a few days off from thinking and begin to journal again by answering the following questions:

- "Do you have clear career or personal goals?" "What are they?"
- "In each area or realm of your life, what is working?" "What is not?"

STEP TWO: ASSESS YOUR ENVIRONMENT

Next, it's important to see if the workspace or home is functional. Ask yourself:

- "Does my space stay organized?"
- "Can I work without getting distracted?"
- "What are my major complaints about my workplace or home?"

STEP THREE: APPLY DESIGN AND FENG SHUI TECHNIQUES

Now it's time to move on to the next level. First, it's important to use intentional design techniques to "solve" the functionality problems in the environment. Feng Shui techniques will balance Nature's elements. Specifically, this means examining the flow of "chi" throughout the space.

Everything is connected in nature and elements of fire, water, wood, earth, and metal all support each other. Centuries ago, the Chinese found that by bringing nature in doors, it could liven up, energize, and create balance / harmony. You want to have all of the elements present in your workspace.

You need to move around the furniture to create a slow meandering traffic flow through a room rather than a straight line. It's an easy picture to imagine. Would you want a raging river or a peaceful stream quietly zigzagging its way through your office? Which do you think would work?

Here's an example of how I applied these steps to help one of my clients and her employees boost company morale and increase company profits: It worked!

STEP 1 – IDENTIFY YOUR GOALS:

My client "Jessica" owns a global consulting firm in the pharmaceutical industry.

During the assessment phase, I discovered Jessica and her employees were operating off an old, outdated business plan, and the mission statement for the company was vague. In addition, everyone in the company felt they were working too hard.

To add to the frustration, Jessica felt she didn't have enough time for a life. No husband, no boyfriend, and no time to find one. Yuck!

The firm was making money, but they needed to have higher profits in order to compete in the marketplace.

This hard working group had a basic idea of the future of the business and what their job descriptions and goals were, but no one considered themselves part of a winning team.

STEP 2 – ASSESS YOUR ENVIRONMENT:

The first thing I asked them to do was to put together a vision statement everyone in the company and any client could understand and support 100%. We posted the vision statement at the reception desk, so now every person could be reminded of why they wanted to work for this company in the first place!

Next, I wanted them to address the open floor plan. The energy was flowing from the front door and right out the back. Energy needed to flow around the workspace and building to support everyone.

The elements in the space were mostly metal and fire; for example, desks, metal beams, lamps, computers and some red walls. These two elements basically cancel each other out; without the other elements, it makes the energy feel, and look, sterile.

There were no plants in the primary work area, no art or mementoes hanging on the walls; many areas were dimly lit, and there was loads of paper!!!

STEP 3 – APPLY DESIGN AND FENG SHUI TECHNIQUES:

Utilizing interior design, I bought trees (which adds the wood and earth elements) and screens to place behind the employees. This broke up the space so the energy moved around the room and not directly out the back door. It also gave the employees some privacy and created fewer distractions for everyone. I also asked each employee to put something on their desk that inspired them. It is important to have objects around you that you love to lift your energy.

I asked Jessica to do the same. She got out all the dusty award plaques the company had earned and placed them behind her desk. We also mixed some of these awards with magnificent art-work to line the long hallway, which led to the main space. This would remind everyone what they had accomplished together.

We organized all the paper clutter into special slots. (This is a simple, but major issue for many! Clear up the mess first!!!) Next we increased Jessica's power by facing her desk to the door. (Always have your back protected!)

We added missing elements to the space, too. To bring water into the balance, a large wall fountain was placed near the reception desk. The door in this area was upgraded, better lighting was added, and new art on the walls was displayed. This gave the impression this company was a bright leader in its field now and in the future.

What were the results? They landed a huge job immediately! The performance of the employees increased, and they admitted they felt "more relaxed" in this working environment. With a solid vision, everyone felt as though they were contributing to a team effort, and attendance at monthly meetings skyrocketed. Lots of fresh ideas moved the company in the positive direction they had wanted to go but had been unable to actualize. Possibly the biggest miracle was Jessica's ability to "focus on her personal life."

This little sprinkle of Feng Shui and Interior Design principles only covers the tip of the iceberg. If you try at least two ideas, you will begin attracting what you want; as you live your life, you will be clear and ready to take advantage of opportunities that you may not have even noticed in the past.

As your business and life changes, your living and work environments will need to change to support your new goals. Pay attention to what your office is saying to you, keep updating your goals, and upgrade the Feng Shui along with it.

Just by reading this, you are on the pathway to prosperity, harmony, and living your life to the fullest!

MADELEINE LA FONTAINE combines over twenty years of experience in Interior Design, Feng Shui and coaching to bring a powerful blend of East, West in creating "inspired spaces for inspired living". A graduate of the Fashion Institute of Design and Merchandising, NBI, and member of the International Feng Shui Guild, Madeleine is available for speaking and consultations. She can be reached direct at 310.339.9975 or visit online at www.inspiredlivingdesigns.com.

CHAPTER 22

Brilliant Business

An Exceptional Formula

KATHLEEN MIERSWA

WOW! WOMEN-OWNED BUSINESSES are growing at twice the rate of all U.S. companies[1]. However, I was taken aback by the statistics that say more than half of women's businesses in 2002 generated less than $50,000 in gross revenues[2]. We need women like you to make more of a difference for yourself financially.

Based on my experience as a financial consultant, I propose using a formula to propel you and your business forward for profitability and greatness. Long-term success is another attribute.

I believe a Brilliant Business is based on universal laws, which serve as silent powerful partners. Spend time developing this formula, which includes values, mission and vision with focus and clarity. Then take the action steps built around specific milestones with gratitude and your silent partners accelerate and leverage results.

THE BRILLIANT FORMULA

The brilliant formula must include the Law of Attraction and the Law of Energy; your silent partners. The Law of Attraction states that if you can see it and believe, you can create it.

The second law supporting the formula is based on the premise that where attention goes, energy flows. The Law of Energy is
connected with the law of attraction. The graph below exemplifies
the Brilliant Business formula. The energy has a circular and back
and forth flow between all three parties; the owner(s), the business
entity and its clients.

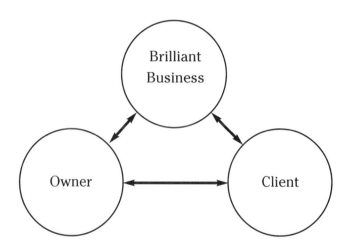

This energy circle feeds itself because of the premise that businesses are an extension of you, the owner. Therefore when making
declarative announcements, I believe you, the owner creates the
basis of brilliance through the Values, Mission and Vision or VMV
process.

Then an action plan, complete with gratitude is called Meta
Mapping. It is more powerful than a strategic plan. The Meta
Mapping process is a very detailed action plan that clarifies and
declares in writing format exactly what you want. Within the plan
are milestones that signify joyful celebrations. This recognition
with the attitude of gratitude inspires your silent partner to compliment your actions. This way you can have fun being in business,
even when there are obstacles.

VALUES

I believe that Values are the foundation for human interactions and therefore business structures. They influence a certain life quality that is the foundation for daily existence. The values you live by knowingly or unknowingly affect your core business structure.

It is essential to take time and clarify your values. The first time sitting down with this process could take some time. However, it is time well spent. Annual value evaluations will take much less time.

Examine the following list of values:

- Achievement
- Accountable
- Ambition
- Assertiveness
- Authenticity
- Balance
- Beauty
- Boldness
- Compassion
- Courage
- Efficiency
- Excite
- Excellence
- Family
- Freedom
- Honesty
- Integrity
- Love
- Loyalty
- Peace
- Spirituality
- Success
- Strength
- Truth

After you prioritize your top five values, explore how you all operate and set rules around these values. Allow any other owner to contribute their values to the process as well. Explain to yourself and others your values and rules. Rules are concrete descriptions, standards and expectations around your values. A person can have the same value but different rules around that value.

For example, my rules of Integrity mean I will keep my word and agreements with regards to time. This can be a challenge especially in LA, where traffic is unpredictable. Planning helps, but if I find myself caught in traffic, I have to call my client and re-negotiate a new meeting time. Otherwise I am breaking my rules about integrity.

I cannot ignore my rules or values as they affect my business. Why? Because, again of my silent partners of attraction and energy. Results flow where energy goes. Breaking rules breaks down brilliant results.

MISSION

After Values, the next step is to create your business mission or purpose statement. A mission or purpose statement serves the values that your business has established. This statement defines how you want to serve your clients.

For example a client's mission statement is as follows:

We make a difference in the world by educating people to leverage wealth principles for financial freedom.

VISION

Having a business vision statement may be first or last in the process step. It doesn't matter. What matters is that the juicier your business dreams are vividly expressed, the more the Laws of Attraction and Energy will be activated.

Using each of your five senses write out your business dreams and vision statement. You must include visual, auditory, kinesthetic, olfactory and gustatory sensory references. These descriptions must be so vivid and virtual that your non-conscious mind will act as if the vision is real and happening NOW!

For brilliant results, construct a picture book or poster boards. Include written clarifying statements about your vision. Make sure your vision board or book includes pictures of you. Go on field trips to fill in any sensory gaps. For example you want a new car or new home, visit a dealership and test-drive your dream car. Go to million dollar open houses and really take in the neighborhood, the construction of the house, and how the house is decorated.

Notice I am using the present tense in the example. Why? You want to activate your silent partner.

"I drive a 2004 silver gray, 5 speed, gray leather 530i BMW with four doors, mobile phone, Bose CD and cassette system with 8 speakers and a Global Positioning System."

In our business seminars, we spend one whole day on Values, Mission and Vision processes. This is a lot of work. However, to have brilliance is like a well-trained athlete. He or she work with values, mission and vision over years and years just to complete a 3-minute Olympic performance.

VMV'S AND META MAPS: THE NITTY GRITTY DETAILS

Once you are finished with your Values, Mission and Vision statements, you will need to create a Meta Map. This step takes your VMV's and puts together a detailed yet powerful action plan.

The Meta Map must detail all end-results, and list all points or milestones in date order. You must have a list of accountable and committed action steps. Assign people and hold them accountable for monitoring their action steps. Make sure you have a list of all inside and outside resources to accomplish these milestones on the dates specified.

Establish action steps that are SMART. SMART means to be Specific, Measurable, Achievable, Risky, Timely. Your silent partner relies on the universal Law of Attraction which in turn requires SMART milestones or action steps.

Below is an example of part of a Meta Map:

MARCH, 2005 MILESTONES
- March 8, Post Feb sales results in employee newsletter
- March 11, Post VMV banner in new office for grand opening event
- March 15, first quarter employee appreciation event at Roy's Restaurant
- March 20, new sales product brochure complete and mailed to top 500 clients
- March 31, $50,000 monthly sales with 30% or $15,000 in profits attained

Having Values, Mission and Vision statements with the Meta Map is excellent. However, a business is brilliant when there are Milestone Celebrations along with a daily attitude of gratitude.

Gratitude Celebrations can be simple and free or as elaborate and expensive as you choose. Take pictures, have awards and line them up in the office; high morale is worth its weight in gold.

Daily gratitude moments along with celebrations communicate to the infinite intelligence that you are a great receiver. This is absolutely brilliant! By being a great giver you will also be a great receiver for unlimited abundance

TAKE ACTION

Take action NOW! You will need focus and discipline, two key ingredients for business profitability and greatness. Do your VMV's and Meta Maps with Gratitude celebration milestones, then have fun and let me know some of your brilliant business results.

KATHLEEN MIERSWA has lived in Europe, Asia, Hawaii, Micronesia, and the mainland US. She has 20 years experience as a senior financial manager analyzing International, Pacific and US businesses. Kathleen pioneered, designed and instructed financial business courses in several languages throughout Asia and the Pacific. She earned her master's degree in clinical transpersonal psychology and is certified in peak performance training. Living in Los Angeles, Kathleen is a California licensed financial consultant. Reach her at KMFinancialGroup@msn.com.

[1] U.S. Department of Labor, 2003
[2] eForum Results, Women Entrepreneurship in the 21st Century, Public Forum Institute, 2003

CHAPTER 23

Heart Of Gold

Bet On Your Heart & Prosper

NATALIE PACE

DIVORCE SUCKS. Your dreams are shattered. Your expenses double. Guilt. You're afraid that only creeps get divorced. (That's your new dating pool, plus, you're one of the creeps). To make the situation worse, you probably can't afford your home anymore.

Unfortunately, it is during a crisis when most of us start thinking about our finances. When you're swimming happily through life, why open 401K statements? They're not bills after all. You can file them directly in the cabinet without fear of debtor's prison.

It might surprise you to learn that the average age of widowhood is 56 (Waddell & Reed, 1997), or that 33-39% of married couples will end up divorced within ten years (National Center for Health Statistics). When a life crisis comes at you, and it will, you will feel so overwhelmed with responsibility, fatigue, hopelessness, time constraints and grief that the temptation to trust in strangers on serious and consequential matters will feel like a matter of necessity. In fact, that is the time to trust your instincts most. That doesn't mean all of your choices will pan out perfectly, but you will be *on the right path*.

Teaching! I thought. I'll be home for my kid after school, and I'll make decent money! How naïve I was. When you consider teachers don't get paid to be at school early, or to stay late and grade papers into the middle of the night, my caregiver was earning more per hour than I was.

Within two years of teaching, I was so far behind on my bills that the county was threatening to put a lien on my one asset—my condominium—in order to collect the property taxes that I owed. My credit card debt had blossomed into a nuclear waste dump that I stored on the top of my refrigerator—so toxic that it made your eyes bleed just to pass by. Needless to say, I was an emotional wreck, and I could only approach the nuclear fallout of which bills to pay, which companies to plead with and which to completely ignore on the nights when my son went with his father. How could I let things get to this point? What kind of world expected me to work all day to pay basic necessities without having a latchkey kid who turned to drugs or television for comfort?

Complaining doesn't pay the bills. I got an executive level position at a nationwide phone company. The salary was double and the hours, though longer on paper, were MUCH less.

At the same time, the wonder of investment cycles began to work in my favor. In 1998, at the time of my divorce, I was locked into a home that I couldn't afford, couldn't sell, and couldn't rent. Real estate had been depressed for most of the 1990s, and my mortgage was underwater, due to a series of Los Angeles disasters—the Rodney King riots, the Malibu fires, mudslides and the Northridge earthquake. (Diversify!) Things were so dire, that, in 1994, you could have bought a home north of Montana for $750,000. (Today you can't buy a termite-ridden hut for under $1.7 million.) By spring 2000, however, the Los Angeles real estate market came roaring back. I borrowed money, gave my crappy little condo a new coat of paint and new carpets and sold it for a small profit.

Burned for nine years by real estate, I turned my eye to Wall Street. You could have thrown a dart at a wall full of stocks and found a winner in 1999, and cocktail parties were abuzz with people touting their gains. When stocks began dipping in 2000, many people considered it a buying opportunity.

On a breezy Santa Monica lunch period, I met with Steven Snappy, a certified financial planner, NASD and SIPC. Steven served up a pie chart telling me if I tossed my real estate profits into a bowl of mutual funds, and dumped in an additional $500/month, I'd churn up a minimum of 12-15% return. "That return," he said in a whisper, behind a cupped hand, "is VERY conservative." (Never mind the fact that I'd have to give up eating to afford the $500 per month!) His mutual fund brochures (which I still have) boasted up to 43.24% returns on funds anchored by AOL, Global Crossing and Enron, to name three. These brochures quoted returns from March of 2000, at the stock market high, something Mr. Snappy neglected to tell me, even though our meeting occurred in September of 2000, after NASDAQ had already tumbled about 40%.

When I met Steven Snappy, I thought P/E was the company in *Erin Brockovich*. I had no idea what Cisco did. I did know, however, that the telecommunications companies were overbooking revenue. I was on the phone daily trying to get hundreds of thousands of dollars worth of credits from a major company that had been over-billing my company at triple the contracted rate for ALMOST A YEAR. If telecommunications companies were cooking the books, what other companies were doing it?

Steven Snappy became very impatient with my questions. It was perfectly easy to see from his charts that the mutual funds he was recommending were amazing, he asserted. By diversifying, I would be protected from the fluctuations of any one sector. How hard was it to see this! Besides, he was making a HUGE, UNAUTHO-RIZED exception for me by lowering the minimum buy-in. If my money sat in savings at 4-5% interest that was less than inflation. We were talking TEN times GAINS in upside potential! Just what was it I didn't understand? (If you ever hear someone talking to you like this, remember s/he is a SALESMAN, not an investment genius! RUN!)

There I was—a professional woman in sharp, new clothes, who had a pen poised to sign a slew of documents I didn't believe in because I wanted some sleazy salesperson to approve of me! Think fast!

Meanwhile Gore was campaigning on eight years of prosperity, and how he was going to be the candidate to continue it! "Not with less than 50% of the vote," I thought. It didn't matter whether Gore or Bush was elected; over 50% of the nation wasn't going to be happy about it. In fact, who could continue eight years of prosperity? And didn't it take a few years for the rookie in office to figure out how to get anything done? How could technology companies, like Amazon.com, operate for YEARS in the red? There were just too many red flags.

Mr. Snappy kept calling and nagging me to sign the documents. I was too busy researching the P/Es, P/E/Gs, Debt/Equity ratios, and 10-Ks of my favorite companies to take his call. I didn't make much money in 2000 in interest, but cash turned out to be the top performing asset class of the 2000 recession. Since then, I've had extraordinary gains in the markets, and founded my own multi-million dollar company.

I'm thrilled I didn't lose all of my money with Steven Snappy, but the most important gain I received that year was confidence. When you have nagging doubts—remember, it's your heart begging for more information. Trust that your uneasy spirit knows something. By prospecting into the heart and soul of your concerns, you will discover USEABLE INFORMATION. Knowledge and wisdom—your own—are better strategies for decision-making than blind trust.

NATALIE PACE is the CEO and founder of I-Sophia, an investment network dedicated to spreading wealth by sharing wisdom. In 2004, Natalie was named #2 Female Entrepreneur. She has been featured on Forbes on Fox, Your World with Neal Cavuto, Good Morning America, Time, USA Today and more. Her exclusive interviews with high-profile business leaders, like Marc Andreessen and Sally Krawcheck, are rated in the top 5 Exec Picks on Forbes.com. www.i-Sophia.com 1.866. I-Sophia. info@WomensInvestmentNetwork.com

CHAPTER 24

Financial Alchemy

Changing Your Relationship With Money!

MORGANA RAE, CPCC, ACC

YOUR CURRENT FINANCIAL SITUATION is a direct reflection of your inner relationship with Money. If you don't like your finances, something needs to change in your relationship. This is where Alchemy comes in.

Alchemy is the art of transformation. With roots in ancient Egypt and classical Greece, Alchemy comes from a time when there was no distinction between science and magic. The mysteries of matter and consciousness were inextricably linked (as they are again, in today's quantum physics). These ancient studies gave birth to modern medicine, psychology, chemistry, and even Sir Isaac Newton's work on gravity.

I've adapted three principles from Alchemist tradition to guide you in transforming your financial reality:

RULE #1: AS IT IS ABOVE, SO IT IS BELOW.

What shows up in your head is going to show up in your life. This chapter will be using fundamental Relationship Coaching skills to help you transform your relationship with money from a dead seed into a flowering garden. A seed comes to life as a living, thriving, fruit-flowering plant. . . in the right environment. So, too, your own prosperity. Your potential for financial abundance is there, waiting for the necessary environment within you. Your relationship with money is like the soil that feeds or starves your economic growth. As long as you have hidden beliefs that cause you to unconsciously repel money, perhaps "protect" yourself from wealth, your garden will not grow.

RULE #2: THERE IS NO SCARCITY.

A wealthy client once explained to me how he had overcome poverty. "The amount of money out there in play every day is limitless, beyond our comprehension. Money is everywhere," he explained. And it's available in proportion to "how big your funnel is to take it in." He had learned to tap into the Source. This relationship supported him.

RULE #3: CONSCIOUSNESS GIVES YOU CHOICE.

I assert even a small change in your relationship consciousness can have a huge impact on your material life. You get what you choose, but first you need to know what you're choosing.

How do I know this? I experienced this transformation myself.

MY STORY:

For years I was struggling as a life coach. I had trouble attracting clients who would pay the fee I wanted. I found myself avoiding discussions of money as long as I could. The whole subject embarrassed me, and my discomfort translated into making clients uncomfortable too. I was "doing" all the right marketing things—

networking, newsletters, sample sessions—and getting nowhere. I was not making a "grown-up" living.

What was in my way, I wondered? My coach and I took a look at my relationship with Money. What were my stories about Money? What is this entity I'm in relationship with? What's going on with this relationship?

Two discoveries popped out: money didn't feel safe or reliable, and money caused separation. (My family would swing between being rich and poor over and over again, and money was a "reason" for family members not to talk to each other for decades.) If my experience of money were given personhood, he'd look like an unkempt, unappealing, Hell's Angel biker type I didn't want to be around. . . someone untrustworthy who liked to cause fights. No wonder I wasn't bringing Money into my life!

This was not the relationship with Money I wanted to have. (And it wasn't the relationship I wanted to model for my clients either.) So I created a new paradigm. I fired the Biker persona and put a romantic, clean-cut, soft-spoken suitor in his place. I chose a new Money "person" to relate to. This Money was like a sweet boyfriend who wooed me with gifts. He even wore a tux! Whenever I received a check, signed a new client, came across some unexpected income, I would graciously thank Money for the lovely gift. And this version of Money was valued and invited into my life.

From then on my business and income kept growing. Within six months I had accrued such a waiting list of clients that I had to add group coaching to my services. I didn't have to look for my new clients; they were finding me. And all I had changed was my inner dialogue with money.

NOW IT'S YOUR TURN:

If you want to improve your financial situation, you must first uncover the beliefs that shaped your relationship with Money.

Get out some paper and respond to these questions. (*Writing creates clarity and speeds your change.*)

- What did you hear about money when you were growing up?
- What beliefs get between you and prosperity?
- What have you heard about women with money?

Next, look at how Money has shown up in your life and in the lives of those around you. Give Money personhood in relationship to you. If Money were a person, what would your version of this Money "person" be like?

- Who is Money? How do you feel about Money? Do you trust Money? Does Money trust you?
- How does Money operate in your life? How does Money feel about you?
- Is Money someone you'd want to have a relationship with if you didn't "have to?"

Now, take a step back and imagine looking at this relationship between yourself and Money-as-a-person from the outside.

- What shift needs to happen in this relationship?

Now, as yourself, negotiate with Money:

- Does Money have a request for you? Do you have a request for Money? What's going to be different?
- How do you want to be different in this relationship? What is the next step to making this change real?

Money is like any other relationship; it comes where it's invited and appreciated. It rarely comes when it is chased. It can be your partner if you listen to it. The more you care for this relationship, the more money you will attract. Here are three final tips:

1. Appreciate money! When a penny shows up on the sidewalk, thank Money for the gift. Don't worry about denomination;

appreciate everything. Think of how good you feel when you are valued for even a small gesture. It's the same for Money. Every time you practice receiving and appreciating, you train the universe to send you more. Show the universe what you value.

2. By now your capacity to receive is growing. You'll notice other stuff creeps in to limit the flow through your funnel to abundance. This stuff may look like clutter, broken appliances, old e-mails, toxic people, time wasters or other energy drains. Clean house! Make space for what you want by having the courage to release what you don't want. You teach the universe how you want to be treated with every choice you make. And nothing gets the universe's attention like saying "No." It's your quickest ticket to miracles.

3. The most important place to make space for what you want is in your head. Clean out fear and pessimism. Plant love and trust instead. Your thoughts are your seeds, and you can grow flowers or weeds. What do you choose to grow?

"Charmed Life Coach" MORGANA RAE helps creative professionals enjoy success without sacrificing their humanity. Clients range from presidents of companies to entrepreneurs, actors, writers, coaches, healers, and women who want something more in their lives. A Certified Professional Coach, Morgana has a background that includes ten years in the entertainment industry, a degree from Smith College, advanced Relationship Coach training, and membership in the International Coaches Federation. Contact: 310 657-5340. Subscribe to FREE monthly newsletter at www.charmedlife-coach.com.

CHAPTER 25

Rich Thinking

AUDREY REED, Ph.D.

YES! I am now a wealthy and successful business woman, author, spiritual being and money expert. This wasn't always the case. If you had told me when I was younger that I would be writing books, seminars and television about the soul of money and your relationship with money, I would have said, this is not my forte. The question of our spiritual relationship with the temporal caused me to peer into my soul and question, how does healing happen?

Once upon a time, I struggled to pay the bills, waited until the last moment to pay some small amount to each vendor and "robbed Peter to pay Paul". I drove an old Ford Mustang that couldn't pass inspection—took the back roads and surface streets everywhere to avoid the police since I couldn't afford the registration fee. (At least I did have insurance since my then three-year-old daughter regularly rode in this vehicle.)

I was driving down a back alley to get home one Saturday afternoon, when to my horror, there in the alley was a police car waving cars past a small accident. I was petrified. I began to say a small silent prayer.

God, *Please help me get through this, please.*

The policeman stopped me and looked at the long passed due red sticker in my window; I began to cry; I had to get to work, I couldn't be late. . . I had to have a car to pick my daughter up at day care, I couldn't couldn't couldn't. . .

This gruff policeman must have had a moment of pity as grace shown down upon me; he said, "Get that piece of junk outta here." And with that, he let me go. Sure I was upset to be driving a piece of junk, but it was the best I could do. Determined to have life and money go better, I began to focus on what we had:

- I started to pay the bills on time.
- I opened them when they came in and said thank you for the electric, for the gas and for the water.
- I got a better job.
- I was grateful.

THE FALLACY — SAFE IN OUR ABUNDANCE!

In the year of 2001 as I snuggled deeply in the security of wealth, I listened to my broker and not my intuition. The stock market tumbled, and I discovered no matter how rich, when the cellular memory of past poverty lurks around the corner, the body's response mechanism kicks in. I found myself, once again not opening bills. As soon as I got a hold of my shock, I took action:

1. Pick up mail each day.
2. Open the bills—say a little prayer over the bill.
3. Pay my vendors. They are my partners for the services they provide. The hard times that helped me through the now times.
4. I said grateful little prayers over each check I wrote.
5. Thankful for the blessing.

We've all had times in our lives when we have wanted to avoid paying bills; we either didn't have the money or wanted to hold onto it a little longer. Financially, money is our safety valve. It is the soft warm fuzzy blanket that says, "You are safe—no one can get you."

Too many people have come into my office with stacks of unpaid bills they just couldn't face opening. One client said, "I don't pay them until the pink bill comes, then I know it's serious, and I have to pay or the vendor will turn off the service." Another client doesn't answer her phone—it's only the bill collectors!

People with lots of money. . . millions of dollars have *the FEAR;* you are not alone.

One of my very wealthy clients advised me she couldn't touch bills. It was as though they burned her hands. She would avoid looking at them or throw them away, thinking I'm Mrs.————, I'm rich, very rich why would the electric company shut off my service? They did, because they didn't know who she was nor did they care. They just knew she hadn't returned any of the calls, and she hadn't paid the bills.

ONE STEP AT A TIME – ONE REALIZATION AT A TIME.

Rich thinking people know they have agreements with their vendors, and they honor them.
1. If you cannot pay the entire bill, pay some of it.
2. Take a percentage from each paycheck to pay every owed vendor.
3. Adjust your thinking from "I am bill paying machine" to "I am paying my vendor; someone who has supplied me with the service I applied for and received. A blessing!"
4. I agreed to pay for the service when they agreed to sign me up for the service.

DOMINO EFFECT – WHAT HAPPENS WHEN WE DON'T PAY OUR VENDORS?

Let's ask the doctor who just saw you on an emergency basis one Friday evening. She stayed in her office after the nurse had left, because you couldn't get there during normal office hours. Now three months later, you still haven't paid her.

If even 30% of her patients did this, don't you think the doctor might have a hard time paying her bills? It is a domino effect!

Call, talk to the vendor, your partner—let them know your situation, and act in partnership with them to get the amount of money you owe paid.

Rich thinking people want to be able to go to the same vendor again and again. So they take good care of the people and service providers that take care of them.

Rich thinking people see everything in their world as an asset and can see the way to use that asset to move them into further abundance.

Jessica and William Nixon were thinking poverty and bankruptcy. They had stopped thinking richly and saw only the debt. Jessica agreed to be on a television money makeover with me on Fox 4 in Dallas. Family Credit Card Debt: $30,000. Three months later they were out of credit card debt and back on the road to financially rich thinking instead of bankruptcy.

1. We shifted their thinking about home money into a business.
2. We examined their assets.
3. Used their banking relationship.
4. Secured a 3-year loan with low interest.
5. Reduced their monthly overhead.
6. The family is talking about money and money issues.
7. The entire family all have individual savings accounts.

The Light and the loving of this abundant world blesses us all. Our Souls are nurtured by the way we perceive our Selves and our world. Thankfulness and focused actions manifest the riches of life.

Be Grateful! Be Blessed.

DR. AUDREY REED—30 years of masterful corporate and entrepreneurial experience. Sold her business in 1994 at 45. Founded Works In Progress, Inc. Audrey's blend of business savvy and spirituality is sought after by organizations, in workshops and with private clients. Prized as a speaker. She is the Money Fitness expert/columnist for MS Fitness Magazine, Direct Selling Women and Money Doctor for Fox 4 Morning TV, Author, "Money ToolBox for Women" and more. E-zine: www.draudreyreed.com, Email: draudreyreed@aol.com (760) 777-6610

⌒

CHAPTER 26

5-Step Proven Strategy

For Delivering A Persuasive Business Presentation That Sells

ARVEE ROBINSON

IN THE EARLY EIGHTIES I worked in corporate America as a consultant. To get business, I gave presentations to prospects in small and large group settings. I spoke a lot. For each presentation, I created elaborate overheads, fancy handouts and delivered—what I thought—was a compelling message. Unfortunately I was not getting my desired results, and for the life of me, I could not figure out why.

One evening I spoke at a prestigious networking group. As usual, I did a great job (or so I thought). After my presentation, a woman with a friendly smile on her face came up to me and asked: "Did you know you said 'okay' after every sentence?" I was mortified. No wonder I wasn't getting the results I wanted. Saying "okay" is so distracting; everyone in my audience must have taken a mental exit.

The very next day, I enrolled in every public speaking class I could find and I joined Toastmasters, an international speaking organization. That was twenty years ago. Today, I help others get more business through persuasive business speaking.

You can learn it too in five easy steps:

STEP 1 – DEVELOP A CLEAR PURPOSE FOR SPEAKING.

If you are a writer, you do not begin to write without first developing a thesis statement. Yet, often when we speak, we forget this crucial step. Consequently, we struggle with what to say and end up rambling. This can be avoided by having a clearly defined purpose statement. There are three parts to creating a purpose statement.

1. *Determine your foremost reason for speaking.* There are six basic reasons for giving a presentation: to inform, persuade, motivate, educate, inspire or entertain. The first four are typically used in business. However, we often make the mistake of choosing "to educate." When we educate our prospects, we give them too much information. If you want to sell more products and services, use "persuade" as your foremost purpose.

2. *Know your audience.* Take the time to do research. How much does your audience know about your products and services? Find out all you can about who you will be speaking to and what is in it for them.

3. *Decide what to give your audience.* Remember this is not what you want; it is about what they want.

The three parts of a purpose statement are:

reason + audience + give = purpose statement.

An example of a purpose statement for this article would look like this:

To motivate women entrepreneurs to give persuasive business presentations so they can close more deals.

STEP 2 – START YOUR PRESENTATION WITH AN ATTENTION GRABBER.

Although there are numerous ways to open a presentation, there are three powerful methods used most effectively in business presentations.

1. *Enrolling questions.* Asking your audience a question immediately gets them involved. It works best if you use closed-end questions. Questions that can be answered with a simple yes or no signified by a raised hand. Prepare your questions ahead of time and practice raising your hand to eliminate any uneasiness in front of your audience. Below are sample enrolling questions asked by an executive recruiter.
    *   "How many people here want to hire the right people?"
    *   "How many people here want to hire the right people and keep them?"

    The beauty of asking enrolling questions is that it engages your audience in both a physical and mental activity. Encouraging these two activities often creates a higher likelihood you will keep your audience's attention throughout your presentation.

2. *Statement of declaration.* A statement of declaration is a great way to begin any speech. When used correctly, this method is so powerful, it literally jerks anyone who may have mentally left the room, right back into their seats.

    For example, one time I heard a speaker begin his speech with "I'm late, I'm late, I'm late!" He said it with such emotion the audience could actually feel his frustration with being late and waited with baited breath to hear more.

3. *Statistical statement.* A statistical statement includes pertinent statistical information of interest to your listeners. A percentage, a number, or a dollar value usually measures this informa-

tion. For example: "80% of communication is non-verbal." When using a statistical statement, do your homework. The information must be 100% accurate. If not, you will lose your credibility and your audience.

It does not matter which one of these "attention grabbers" you use to begin your presentation. Experiment using different types and see which one works best for you. Just remember, your opening statement or question must be relevant to your topic and appropriate for your audience. If you grab your audience's attention in the beginning, chances are you will keep it until the end.

STEP 3 – THE MEAT IS IN THE MIDDLE.

We have all heard people buy on emotion. Which emotion? Studies show the number one emotion people buy on is fear. So why not use it in your business presentations? Instead of telling your prospects the great things you can do for them, find out what they are afraid of and tell them how you can help.

Ask questions to prepare for your audience. Learn more about what problems they need solved, and what problems they most fear. Everyone has a problem to be solved. Find out what it is and let them know you have the solution.

When presenting your solution, keep it simple. Avoid jargon and offer specific steps to a solution.

STEP 4 – USE POWERFUL BODY LANGUAGE.

Since 80% of all communication is non-verbal, use your body to support your words. One of the best ways to do this is a strong stance. If at all possible, stand while making a presentation.

Standing will open the diaphragm so your voice will project further and command attention. Stand with your legs shoulder length apart in the "rooted position". This position will keep you from swaying, rocking or pacing, all of which are distracting to your audience.

STEP 5 – END WITH A BANG!

End your presentation as strong as you began. There are three parts to a powerful close.

1. *Q & A session.* If you have a question and answer session, ask a colleague to have a question prepared ahead of time. This will give the audience time to formulate questions and eliminate a potential awkward silence.

2. *Call to action.* Invite your audience to call you, email you, or sign on the dotted line. Give away free stuff in exchange for a business card. Whatever you do, make it clear what you want your audience to do.

3 *Closing statement or memorable close.* This statement is your last word. Think about what thoughts and feelings you want to leave with your audience. Never end your presentation with "thank-you". After the great information you gave your audience and the solution you provided to their problem, they should be thanking you. Always end with a strong word or phase.

This five-step system can be used for any type of business presentation. Use it for your thirty-second introduction, a twenty minute round table discussion or a full-blown on-stage sales presentation. By using this easy approach to persuasive business presentations, you will close more deals than ever before.

ARVEE ROBINSON, a Persuasive Speaking Coach, works with Service Professionals and Small Business Owners who rely on group presentations for generating new business. Arvee teaches them a simple, proven 5-step system to instantly speak like a pro. Since 1997 she has helped hundreds of individuals eliminate nervousness, command audience attention as well as develop and deliver sales-winning presentations. For free tips and articles on improving your speaking skills go to www.arveerobinson.com or call 909-626-5521.

CHAPTER 27

Lions And Tigers And Process. . . Oh My!

BETH SCHNEIDER

WE'VE ALL BEEN THERE—paper piled to the ceiling, phone ringing off the hook, email box so full AOL is complaining that you've filled up the server.

Everyone knows how hard you work.

So why is it there are just never enough hours in the day? You know you are great at what you do, but have you ever stopped to think about how you do things? In what order? And why? Have you ever really thought about the day-to-day processes you follow? Well, you should.

The scary statistic is that 80% of businesses fail within the first five years. Part of the reason the failure rate is so high is that many entrepreneurs don't treat their business like a business.

Many are resistant to planning and creating processes because they think it is tedious and boring, but it doesn't have to be.

Taking the time to think about your day-to-day operations will make your business more consistent and efficient; it will save you time and inevitably make you more money. And here's the kicker: all with *less* effort.

STEP 1 – IDENTIFY WHAT YOU NEED

First, you have to figure out which processes you need. Start by creating a list of tasks. Some common ones include: invoicing, creating proposals, marketing, networking, etc. Create your own list by thinking about what you do on a daily, weekly and yearly basis. Make a list of everything you do as far as your job is concerned.

Next, make a wish list of things you want to be doing. Your wish list may include things like: getting more clients, buying a better computer, starting an e-zine, building a website, etc.

Once you have your lists, prioritize and choose what to work on first. Decide what your main goal is. Are you looking to get more clients? If so, focus on the tasks that will do just that, such as networking, writing proposals, etc.

If your goal is to delegate, focus on the tasks you can develop and then give away.

STEP 2 – CREATING PURPOSE FOR YOUR TASK

Have you ever been around a child that constantly asks "Why, why, why?" Yes, sometimes it can be trying, but asking "Why?" actually makes sense. Specify and understand for yourself why you are doing something. Imagine asking for driving directions. You have to know where your starting and ending points are. If you don't, you are just driving in circles. You never know if you are "there" yet, because you have no idea where "there" is.

For the task or tasks you are focusing on, define specific end results. Ask yourself, why am I doing this task? What should my end accomplishment be? When should I complete this? How will my customer be benefited? How will I be benefited? How will I know it has worked?

I was talking to a woman at a networking meeting one night, and I asked her what her purpose for being there was. She was very clear: she wanted people to sign-up to hold cosmetics parties in their homes, and she had realized her process did not support her goal. Sometimes people signed up, but more often than not, she left the meeting empty handed. She had the opportunity to look at how she was trying to sell the parties, and she made some changes to her networking process. Soon she had doubled the number of parties being booked.

STEP 3 – DOCUMENTING YOUR PROCESS

Consultants charging upwards of $100/hour use a method called flowcharting.

A flowchart is a visual blueprint of a process. Different shapes are used to indicate the step-by-step procedure being followed. There are a few common shapes.

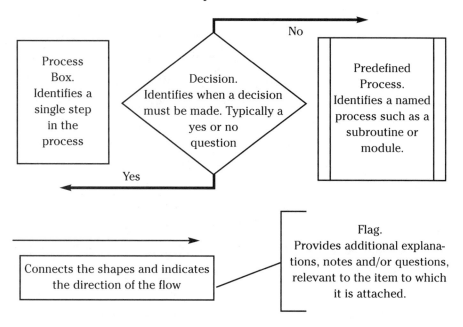

These shapes are linked together to form the process. There are many ways to use flowcharts, but we are going to address capturing the current or "as-is" process.

Capturing the "as-is" process gives you the opportunity to take a detailed look at how you are completing a task. For instance, one of my clients had experienced some turnover in the administrative department. They were paying their bills, but no one was managing their vendor accounts. We documented what little process there was, and together, expanded the process to achieve their goal of updating and managing their accounts.

Yes, you can do this; just try it.

There are many flowcharting software programs. You don't need to buy expensive software to capture your process. All you need is a packet of Post-it notes and a table or a wall.

Say you want to document your networking process. Ask yourself, "Where does this start?" "What trigger do I receive to know there is a meeting?" "How do I find out about a meeting?" Let's assume the answer is you get an email notification. You would write, "Receive email invite" on your first sticky note. That note goes on the wall. Continue asking yourself, "What happens next?" "What is the next step I am to do ?" The answer goes on the next sticky note, and it is placed next to the first item on the wall. Continue this until the process ends.

Be aware of your decisions' points. These are most commonly found when you find yourself saying (or thinking) things such as, "it depends" or "yeah, but".

The idea is to be aware of and capture information that differs because of the circumstance. Think about making phone calls. If the person answers, you follow one set of steps. Your sticky notes may read, "Set an appointment," "Note appointment in calendar," "Tell assistant to prepare forms for meeting."

If the person does not answer, your steps are completely different. Instead of "Set an appointment," your sticky may read, "Leave a message," "Note in a calendar to call again in two days."

To capture this on stickies, you start with the question, "Was the person reached?" You create two lines of sticky notes, one set of steps you follow if the answer is 'yes', and another if the answer is 'no.' This is a great tool to see where you might have holes in your process.

Make sure your sticky notes are clear and include a specific action. Six months from now, you will want to know what you meant by each one. If you forgot a step or think of something later, just move the sticky notes around. It's actually fun.

Once your "as-is" process is on the wall, ask yourself if the purpose is being met. If not, you will need to add or delete some steps to make it more productive and goal-oriented.

STEP 4 – IMPROVING YOUR PROCESS

Don't be afraid of planning and organization. Once a flowchart is complete, you have a map. This visual blueprint can be evaluated for shortcuts, bottlenecks and what I call "La-La land" and "Roundabouts".

"La-La land" is just code for things falling through the cracks, the left hand not talking to the right hand, dropping the ball, etc. The idea is to identify the holes before something goes wrong. Read through the process and ask yourself, "Might I forget about this?" "Could something get lost here?"

"Roundabouts" are steps that overlap. For example, when you keep going back to something you have already done or could have completed all at once. One of my clients is an engineering company that deals with Industrial Laboratory ovens. We documented their estimate preparation "as-is" process, and we determined sometimes a customer was called four times before an estimate was completed. They were going around and around the information they needed.

To remedy this, they created one detailed order-form that anyone in the office could fill out. They cut down the estimate processing time from 4 to 6 days to less than 24 hours, all by looking at steps on sticky notes.

Are you making this same kind of mistake? It took me six months to convince this particular client to do this exercise. Two hours later, they were on their way to a 400% productivity increase, and they are still thanking me for being so persistent.

Good luck and happy charting!

BETH SCHNEIDER is the Chief Infopreneur of Process Prodigy, a seminar and consulting company that shows entrepreneurs how to develop the behind the scenes processes and systems they need to support their business and keep their clients. When busy entrepreneurs feel like they are stuck on a hamster wheel, running faster and faster, but not getting anywhere, they turn to Beth for help. For seminar schedules or product information, visit www.processprodigy.com or call us at 888-584-5452.

PART III

SPIRITUAL FULFILLMENT

CHAPTER 28

Your Inner World Creates Your Outer Reality

LILLIAN BAJOR

SOFTEN YOUR GAZE as you read this paragraph and shift your awareness inside—become aware of your breath. Watch the subtle changes in your chest and abdomen as you take a few deep breaths. Relax and become aware of your thoughts, don't judge them—just notice what you are thinking. In a moment, gently close your eyes and become aware of the content of your consciousness. What are you thinking?

Just notice and return your attention to your breath. What are you feeling? Again notice without judging, and return your awareness to your breath. What bodily sensations are you experiencing? Relax and breathe into any tightness and return your attention to your breath. Now for the next three minutes, close your eyes and be fully present in your inner world.

Take a moment to jot down your experience. This is an exercise in awareness. The most important relationship in your life that defines and creates all your other relationships is the one you have with yourself. In order to deeply "know thyself" and what your life is about are questions that can only be answered by you; you must go within.

The intense energy of the fast-paced world we live in doesn't support taking time to explore the inner life. The world is constantly pulling at your awareness and senses taking you outside of yourself so your focus becomes external. This makes it appear that the solutions you are looking for, your source of happiness and fulfillment are all somewhere out there and have nothing to do with what's inside of you.

This is false and disempowering since it takes you in the wrong direction, away from your center, disconnecting you from your true source within.

The practice of meditation will take you on a journey to your higher self. All the wisdom, inspiration and guidance you need are available to you through meditation. It is important to have right understanding when meditating; that is, meditate to unify with your higher self. That is right identification, connect with your inner source. You are not your thoughts, feelings or sensations that are moving through your consciousness; you are that which is aware of your thoughts, feelings and sensations.

In truth, you are pure awareness and to realize and experience this is the purpose of meditation. Watching your breath is one way to get you there. In meditation, you are also turning away from the illusion that the *only* reality is the one you see and experience with your eyes and senses.

Being true to myself did not come naturally to me. I had to work for many years to find my own truth—to discover what is really important to me and what I wanted from life. I carried mixed messages inside of me that I had to sort through on many levels. The material world made everything seem separate and apart from me. Life seemed chaotic—a struggle and the underlying message was you have to work hard to survive. However, through meditation, I became aware in the natural world, life is interdependent. There is order, harmony and divine cooperation. All of nature reflects incredible beauty, vastness and abundance everywhere, a perfect flow—nature doesn't struggle.

It was only through my spiritual practices that I realized and experienced the truth, we are not separate, powerless or limited in any way. We are ONE beyond what the mind can comprehend. We have a profound connection on the invisible side of life. We can change our world by changing our reality from the inside out.

These are spiritual practices that helped me find my truth and change my life from the inside out. The journey is ongoing and infinite in its rewards.

Meditation helped me to release outer focus and gave me the strength to follow my own path and explore my own truth. I realized living an authentic life was a high value for me. I discovered I am my own source; I create my own reality with my thoughts, feelings and actions. I learned as I change and grow, my reality changes with me and adjust to my new level of awareness. A valuable practice I learned to help me change old patterns of thought is working with affirmations.

Affirmations can help you change your inner world of thoughts and beliefs that are outdated and no longer supportive of you. As you become aware of habitual thoughts that are unproductive, jot them down and create an affirmation that is the opposite. Affirmations are meant to be positive statements, stated in the present tense—they are fueled by emotion. Positive uplifting emotions like love, passion and joy, combined with a heartfelt affirmation will bring you great results.

Be patient with yourself as you work in consciousness to change your inner world of thoughts and core beliefs. At times, it may seem you are experiencing the opposite of the change you are working to create; as old patterns of thought are releasing, they move through your awareness.

Be compassionate with yourself. These old beliefs have been with you for many years. Judging and criticizing only perpetuate a negative cycle and keep you stuck. Compassion, understanding and practicing loving kindness with yourself will quicken the process of release and create a space where transformation can and does happen.

I became aware that there was a cycle to my process which required deep self-love and letting go. At times like this, prayer is the sweetest surrender.

Prayer is a powerful practice of surrendering, letting go of struggle and acknowledging the Universal Intelligence that created, sustains and maintains this Universe. By acknowledging a higher power in your life you open yourself to miracles. By letting go, you release effort and become receptive to God's grace. Great faith can move mountains. The essence of answered prayer is, "Believe first and then you will see."

Another great practice to create change is visualization, which is creating a clear picture in your mind's eye of your goal and being unwavering in your focus. See the reality you want for yourself in your mind, especially when the outward appearance seems contradictory to what you are envisioning for yourself; this is when these practices support you and pull you through to attain your goal.

Believing in myself and loving myself are the two pillars that help me through all the challenges that are my life lessons. I used to wish my challenges in life would go away. I thought if I could get to the end of the journey, then I would be happy. But then I realized I was misunderstanding the value of my challenges. I realized my challenges made me strong and took me deeper into myself to a greater realization of truth.

This path takes determination and commitment. Honoring my truth and myself is something I had to learn and continue to work with. I encourage you to embrace your life lessons, challenges and joys with a new awareness, realizing what you see outside is only half of the whole, and the invisible side of life is as real as the visible. Be willing to be different in your life and with yourself, listen from a new place; acknowledge what you carry within you every step of the way.

Remember to love yourself and appreciate who you are. Celebrate your uniqueness and find your source within. You are the center from which all things flow.

LILLIAN BAJOR is a graduate of University of Santa Monica in Applied Spiritual Psychology, a Practitioner of Science of Mind since 1995 and practicing Siddha Yoga Meditation since 1999. Lillian's quest is to bridge the world of material reality with spiritual truth. She coaches individuals and groups to connect the spiritual and practical aspects of money to create lasting wealth with joy. You can visit her at www.LillianBajor.com and sign up for her free E-zine.

CHAPTER 29

It Can't Be An Accident If You Do It On Purpose

Six Steps To Getting Anything You Want, Whenever You Want It

STEPHANIE FRANK

HAVE YOU EVER HAD a time in your life when things were going really well? I mean really well? Effortlessly, as if by accident, you wish for something and the right people, the right circumstances and resources show up. You easily reach a goal that once seemed impossible. It almost seems like a dream—a fleeting moment of luck. What if you could harness that ability whenever you want to achieve anything you want in your life? Imagine. . . more focus, money, freedom and fun could be yours for the asking. Would you learn the secret? Would you use it?

Successful people attract abundance into their lives with purpose and intention. It is the secret that all people who maintain success and prosperity in their lives share. It's a secret that many don't talk about openly. Why? Most people believe that working harder, longer and with more effort is the key to great success, and they don't believe that success could come any other way. After all, isn't that what we were all taught in school? Get a great education, go to college, and get a job. Well, let's face it—it's not working so well is it?

The truth is I experienced a lot of financial success at an early age. Millions of dollars came into my life. I worked hard to grow a multi-million dollar business. After all, grow a bigger business is the goal, right? Wrong. The pursuit of success led me to an unbalanced approach to life. Work hard, no play, go in early and leave late became my mantra.

I couldn't take it. It had to stop. Somewhere there was a key to finding the balance I craved. But where? Who could tell me the secret? How did successful people have it all—a profitable business, health, family and free time? I asked every successful person I knew to tell me the secret. They all told me that true success comes from mastering the skill of manifesting—bringing into reality the things that you want using your mind. In essence, it is about using the infinite resources of energy, the Universe, to assist you in your quest.

Could it really be true? Could anyone manifest his or her own version of success on a continuous, repetitive and consistent basis? Was there really an infinite source of energy and knowledge, just waiting to help me? I had to find out, and I had nothing to lose. So I practiced, learned, and great things happened. Today this powerful system is an integral part of my everyday life, and I am proud to share it with you. Do you want great things to happen to you too? Start here and they will.

STEP 1 – MAKE A DECISION TO HAVE WHAT YOU WANT, WHEN YOU WANT IT.

This is deceptively simple. It would seem that making the decision to have whatever you want would be easy, but most people are tentative when it comes to being specific. People say things like "It would be nice if. . . " and "We'll see what happens when. . . ". It won't work. First, you must state that "I am in the process of. . . " or "I will be" when making a decision. Make sure you're clear on when you will receive the results. You must be resolute, and allow no one (not even yourself) to undermine your confidence in your decision.

So what do you want? Start thinking and practicing now. Here are a couple of practice sentences to get you started.

- I am in the process of becoming a millionaire by the time I am 50.
- I will be living a life of personal and financial freedom on or before my 45th birthday.
- I am going to have a weeklong Italian vacation in 2005.

Start small. "I'm having chicken for lunch today" is a very decisive statement. "I am going on vacation in Los Angeles for a week in June" is also decisive. Once you have practiced and mastered this decisive language, you are ready to move on to Step 2.

STEP 2 – BE CLEAR ABOUT THE OUTCOME.

The next step is to be extremely clear about the details of the outcome. This is done in the context of what you DO want, not what you DON'T want. Practice visualizing yourself in the situation you want to create. How do you do this? Once again, the simplest way is to start small.

Think about this: when ordering a salad in a restaurant, you choose the type of lettuce, vegetables, cheese and dressing. You visualize how the salad will look when it arrives at your table. You are clear about what you want. After all, when you're thinking about the salad, you don't have a visual picture of a chicken sandwich in your mind, do you? Of course not! You have a visual image of the salad you wish to eat. It works the same with bigger items, like financial freedom. You must visualize the money, the bank statements, investments or just plain truckloads of money arriving into your life.

STEP 3 – DETACH FROM THE PROCESS.

One thing that holds many people back is not knowing "how" to do something. Forget it. The "how to do it" instructions will appear after you have clearly defined what you want.

Take the example of ordering the salad. After you order, you don't have to worry about how the salad will take shape. Every restaurant prepares salad differently, but the outcome is the same—it arrives at your table ready to eat. It is the same with all other events in your life.

STEP 4 – EXPECT THAT IT WILL HAPPEN.

Now that you're decisive and clear about what you want and not trying to control the process, set an expectation that what you want will in fact appear. It may not appear in the way you thought or at the precise time. Possibilities you thought were a sure thing may disappear. In fact, you may even experience frustration, anxiety or impatience trying to control the outcome. Ask yourself "what lesson could I learn from this experience" and turn it into a personal growth opportunity.

STEP 5 – BE OPEN TO POSSIBILITY.

As I mentioned in the last step, the path to the outcome may (and probably will) show up in ways you never imagined before. It is your job to explore possibility. Suspend judgment of how things should be done based on your past experiences and ask yourself "Is the situation, person or resource that is in front of me supposed to help me on my journey? If so, how?" When you ask the question, you will be given the answers—one step at a time.

STEP 6 – PRACTICE GRATITUDE.

Are you thankful for the things you have in your life right now? Do you look at your challenges as an opportunity to grow or a burden that needs to be eliminated? When you practice being thankful for specific events in your life, including the burdens, even when you don't understand why they appear in your life, your ability to manifest accelerates almost to the speed of thought.

Practicing these steps means taking action, being consistent and being open to change. Getting what you want does not always mean that it is easy. Challenges occur. Emotions, other people's negative views and comments set you back. But in the end, it all comes back down to your choice. Choose to get what you want and it will happen for you. That's a promise. Guaranteed.

For over 15 years, STEPHANIE FRANK, "The Accidental Millionaire", founder of The Rich Living Worldwide Community for Empowering Entrepreneurs has been helping people grow their business without losing their mind. After making her first million at the age of 22, she has inspired and led thousands of entrepreneurs down the path toward abundant wealth. She helps entrepreneurs have more focus, sales, freedom and fun. Become a community guest or learn more at www.StephanieFrank.com

CHAPTER 30

Manifesting Made Easy

DEBBIE FRIEDMAN, C.Ht.

ARE YOU READY TO MANIFEST TRUE WEALTH and success in your life?

Whether we know it or not and whether we like it or not, we are continuously manifesting all aspects of our lives through our thoughts and feelings. What we focus on, what we give great emotional feeling to, is created in the Universe to support these intentional or unconscious desires.

You have the power to bring into your life whatever you choose. If you are conscious about your choices and use the power that has been given to you, you can manifest the life of your dreams.

If, however, you are unconscious in your choosing, you may be unpleasantly surprised to find that you have created quite a different result.

The practical dilemma for many of us is that we don't know how to use the power we have.

Ask yourself now: "Am I manifesting all the health, wealth, success, and prosperity I want in my life?" Look around you and you'll find the answer.

More than ever, NOW is the time to learn how to use your powers correctly, wisely, and productively. NOW is the time to begin to use, consciously, what you might have been using unconsciously in the past. NOW is the time to create the life you desire and deserve!

I'm going to share a simple step-by-step process with you for manifesting this magic in your life. Here are some keys to remember before we begin— it's simple, but may not be easy at first. Once you become practiced with this process, you will do it automatically. The secret to manifesting successfully lies in the sequence of the step-by-step process.

Most important to remember is that this really works. It really does!

GETTING STARTED

1. GET INTO A STATE OF SPIRITUAL VIBRATION.

As a starting point, begin by creating the right environment for success, ready to transmit the energy of what you choose for your life out into the Universe so that it can respond.

Go to an area where you can be quiet for a period of time. Find a comfortable place to rest and support your body completely. Close your eyes and begin by taking several deep breaths to relax your body, calm your emotions and clear your mind. Feel your body relaxing as you breathe. Inhale peace and exhale any negativity or stress.

It is generally best to invite whatever force of universal energy you choose to surround you. You may call this force God, Buddha, Jesus, Spirit, Life Force, Angels, Higher Power or Divine Presence.

There are many ways to get into a state of spiritual vibration. The simplest way is to imagine a beam of golden or white light coming down and surrounding you completely. Allow the light to move into you, through you, and around you. Become aware that you are surrounded and gently protected.

2. CHOOSE WHAT YOU DESIRE.

First of all, know that what you desire has already been chosen for you. You have the desire for a reason, and the desire needs to be expressed in the world. We all have a purpose to be fulfilled in life, and our desires are the signs that show us the way of our own path. Be clear, specific, and definite with your choices.

Visualize or imagine a white screen in your mind's eye. See the words "I Choose" in front of you and write out what you choose to experience in your life at the present time in your own handwriting.

Focus on each word and let each word become deeply impressed in your mind. Accept the fulfillment of your desire NOW, not tomorrow or sometime in the future. Say to yourself silently, "I accept the fulfillment of this desire NOW."

3. EXPECT THE GIFT.

Because the desires you have are there for a reason and because the Universe is friendly to your plans, know that what you've chosen is coming to you.

Because you have already accepted the fulfillment of your desire, expect that your desires will be fulfilled.

Love the feeling of having what you have chosen.

4. VISUALIZE WHAT YOU DESIRE.

Visualizing is a key ingredient to manifesting. Look at the white screen in your mind's eye again and begin to run a movie of what you have chosen. See yourself doing, being, having, and enjoying your good in overflowing measure. See yourself being happy, joyous, loving, free, and prosperous. Add color, depth, sound, and texture to your vision.

Feel the excitement of seeing your desire already fulfilled. See it, feel it, taste it, touch it, smell it, sense it, know it. Use all of your senses and let your vision become etched in your mind in detail, knowing what you are seeing is the present time.

5. LOVE WHAT YOU SEE.

Love is the strongest emotional vibration; nothing is more powerful than the power of love. Allow the power of love to work for you.

As you watch the vision of your desires fulfilled, say to yourself silently, "I love what I see." Let all the love you can feel in your heart pour out as you focus on the beautiful images of what you have chosen.

Love the pictures of total fulfillment that you are seeing in your mind and feeling in your heart.

6. KNOW YOUR DESIRES ARE BEING FULFILLED.

Here, you move beyond believing and into the knowing that what you desire is being fulfilled. This is the certainty that makes all the difference. Say to yourself silently, "Let there be total fulfillment now."

Allow yourself to receive everything you desire. Your faith in the loving support of the Universe is powerful. Know, with certainty, that your good is coming into visible form and experience. Your good is coming to you by the power of your word. Say to yourself silently now, "It is done and so it is."

7. SURRENDER.

Now is the time to tap into the power of the Universe and allow Divine Spirit to be the only power at work in your life. Let go and let God. Release your needs and desires. Be willing to receive your highest and greatest good. Know that only that which is perfect, plentiful, good, beautiful, loving, peaceful, and joyful is now manifesting in your world.

8. EXPRESS GRATITUDE.

Express gratitude for all you have received. Let your heart overflow with joy and gratitude. Thank God with praise and love.

Become thankful for your total fulfillment now, as thankful in this moment as you will be when your desire is fully established in visible form.

9. TAKE THE APPROPRIATE ACTIONS IN YOUR WORLD.

Move into action in your word as co-creator with your Higher Power. Listen to your inner guides and do what is in front of you to the very best of your ability. Move forward with faith that you are being guided in your daily life.

Do what you feel inspired to do. Trust your intuition and trust your guidance. Stay open to the miraculous moments that will be unfolding each and every day. Look forward with anticipation to these miracles and become grateful as they appear in your life.

As you experience manifesting success and begin to consciously create, you lose all worry, doubt, and fear because you know you have the power to create every aspect of your life. You are now free to open your arms to receive your abundance with joy, peace, ease, grace, and love.

May you create the life of your dreams, the life you desire and deserve!

DEBBIE FRIEDMAN, C.Ht., is a speaker and certified Clinical Hypnotherapist with more than 20 years in the field. She is the creator of the popular Cleaning Out the Closet of Your Mind for Wealth series, and the Manifesting: The Step-by-Step Process for the Secret of Success CD and book series. Her office and private practice are in Southern California where she conducts workshops, seminars, and teleconferences. Debbie may be contacted at (310) 230-0872 or www.CleaningOutTheCloset.com

CHAPTER 31

Living In The Absence Of Fear

LISA HAISHA

I ARRIVED A FEW HOURS AGO at my Hungarian hotel feeling a bit lonely. A job I was working on just ended, and I felt the need to take time out to figure out what to do next. Although I have traveled extensively, this was my first trip alone, which brought out a lot of uncomfortable emotions; everything from fear of going places alone and having no one to share my experiences with, to getting assaulted, as a single woman. I have four days here to relax before I meet up with a friend in Prague, and I've decided to make the most of it, dive into a different culture and see what happens.

I've learned the city of Budapest is divided into two main sections: Buda and Pest, separated by the broad Danube River.

I decided to stay on the Pest side, which is livelier, and I also decided my first priority while there is to visit the bathhouses of Budapest. Apparently, the largest bathhouse of its kind is located in Szechenyi— visited by two million visitors each year. *Szechenyi* (*Chech-nee*). I like the sound of the word.

Armed with directions and information about what to take— bathing suit, bath towel, and toiletries—I was off to the Metro. I buy a ticket, and board the charming little train they call the subway, open for adventure.

As in so many cities filled with regular commuters going about their habitual routines, the train is filled with blank faces and lost souls. I see an empty seat.

Just as I'm about to sit down, the train jolts, and I stumble and fall into the cushiony lap of a large old woman. Embarrassed, I give her a big hug and joke, "Hi Grandma, I've missed you!" She looks at me as if I'm nuts; other passengers look on with curiosity, and I pull away and manage to plant myself in the seat across from her. Humiliated, I start to laugh. Then "Grandma" joins me. Her laugh brightens her whole face.

She takes a moment to look me over. I do the same to her. Then she reaches out with a freckled, wrinkled hand; and I give her mine. She looks at me lovingly; her turquoise eyes still have their youth, and her broad face and yellow-toothed smile light up the subway. I see other passengers smiling—a few, anyway, waking up. After a few more stops, we come to her destination. She squeezes my hand—no words are needed—then reaches behind her neck and unclasps a chain around her neck, holding a gold cross. She puts the necklace into my hand and folds my fingers around it tightly. Then she tilts her head down and kisses my folded fist.

I don't know what to do or say. I look at her eyes, welling up with tears. My tears follow. She struggles to rise, and I help her to step off the train. She looks at me, as if I were a granddaughter she hadn't seen in years, the way my real grandmother would have if she were still alive.

I close my eyes and listen to the melodic clicking and squeaking of the train on the tracks. The romantic scent of "grandmother's" perfume still permeates the still air. Perhaps this is why I felt an intuitive urge to go.

Given the old woman's response, I don't believe she had been hugged in a long time. My falling into her lap doesn't, in retrospect,

seem an accident for either one of us. In fact, it felt like a small miracle, a divine intervention. I'd been melancholy and homesick. Maybe,
she was, too. If we could just realize how interconnected we all are
spiritually, then we might treat each other completely differently. I
put the necklace around my neck as a reminder of her loving energy.

I sense my stop is fast approaching, and I slowly open my eyes
and step onto the platform.

A massive mustard-yellow building looms in front of me. It
boasts towering pillars and a portico adorned with sculptures and
a stunning art-nouveau mosaic. This must be Szechenyi—the most
elegant public bath I could ever have imagined.

As I enter the vast complex, I walk directly to an open window
overlooking the huge pools outside. I look out at a comforting mist
of steam, simmering above the waters to see bathers, relaxing in
pleasurable lassitude in the thermal baths. It's a healthful *dolce
vita,* Budapest style. I witness lovers nuzzling, potbellied men on
benches with half their expansive buttocks hanging out of small,
tight bathing suits, while others play chess on cork-chessboards
floating on the calm water. I feel like a time-traveler transported to
the sixteenth century in ancient Rome.

An attendant escorts me to the woman's locker room. I enter,
and find myself standing in a small, dingy room that smells of stale
sweat—vintage locker room. I undress and put my belongings in a
safe locker.

In contrast to the United States—especially southern
California, which I call home—nobody seems self-conscious of his
or her body. I'm in one of my less-than-svelte phases at present,
and in Los Angeles, my inner voice would chastise me for not being
a twig, but compared to most of the women here, I feel positively
sexy and flaunt my body, every pound of it. I look into the mirror,
"Uh-huh— one bodacious babe."

Everyone seems anxious to get into the water. We trade side-
ways glances, but no one makes eye contact or talks—the way

people act on elevators. I finish putting on my black one-piece bathing suit, and gingerly transfer my feet from shoes to sandals in order to avoid one of the many varieties of fungus I'm sure must thrive on the floors here.

Excited, I head for the pools. The hovering steam seems inviting. Men and woman of all ages soak in a communal "ahhhhhhh." I set down my hotel towel and slip into the warm thermal water. Even with twenty people in the pool and another ten lounging on chairs or benches, it seems relatively empty and private. I feel like I have the place to myself. My body luxuriates as I relax and sink naturally into a meditative reverie.

I close my eyes and tilt my head back on the cement rim of the pool, facing the blue sky and floating clouds as I drift, soaking in the warmth of the sun's rays.

Suddenly, a green and purple elephant, sporting Dolce and Gabana stilettos, featuring a big blood-red flower on the toe, flies above me. A twinge of jealousy flows through my body, as I think, "I would look great in those shoes." As my gaze rises above them, I notice a woman riding the elephant and rub my eyes in astonishment as I realize it's "Grandma" from the subway! She smiles and waves, calling out, "There's no place like home!" as the elephant flies up through the clear blue sky.

I come out of my daydream, open my eyes with a jolt and look around: Everything is back to normal. I look around and see only bathers enjoying their afternoon in the peace and calm.

I think about how wonderful it is to be able to relax enough to release fear and embrace unusual experiences, even in daydreams. Grandma, who will live with me forever, has taught me that we are all connected. We could all live richer lives and fill the emptiness in most of our souls if we could only release the fear that prevents us from connecting to others.

LISA is an LA based writer/director/producer. She also holds a Masters in spiritual psychology. She has been traveling extensively to over fifty countries around the world for over a decade, including a long stay in Tokyo, where she modeled and acted. While traveling, she had weeklong intensive stays in the Ashrams of Kyoto to the caves of Petra. For more information please visit her website at www.lisahaisha.com or email her at moshimush@aol.com.

CHAPTER 32

Spirituality In Business

RACHEL E. HART

"True happiness comes not from a limited concern for one's own well-being, or that of those one feels close to, but from developing love and compassion for all sentient beings."
—Dali Lama

YOU ARE A COMBINATION of body, mind and soul, and it is natural that spirit manifest through you and your business. This takes place through different ways—from letting spirit guide you, spiritual practices in business and/or being spirited to get the job done.

Go within and connect with spirit, and it will guide you. This doesn't mean you are meditating all day, but a balanced approach will serve you very well. Using your spirituality and intuition is something you can call upon to help you navigate through the ups and downs of life and business.

One of my clients bought an art store. She had no prior experience in this business. She was situated in a building where she could not advertise, and she was panicking. I suggested she meditate with a mala (prayer bead) when she started to feel insecure or started thinking negatively. She would move the beads of the mala over her index finger (Jupiter finger for self-knowledge, prosperity and intuition) and recite a mantra (any spoken or unspoken word) to stop the negative thoughts. After a few months she called me and said, "No one will be in the store, and I will start meditating with my mala and people will come in." Her business kept growing with each quarter, and she told me a year later "A day without meditating with her mala was like a day not connecting with infinity."

The mind has built-in safeguards. The first thought will naturally be negative to help protect you and avoid negative consequences. When a negative thought comes up; think the opposite positive thought. When you see both negative and positive, you are neutral, and this is were things start to manifest. This can be done as a mental exercise, which takes a lot of self-observation and mental control, or you can stop the negative thought by meditating with a mala.

Sometimes it is best to push through while at other times, it is better to let things come to you and be in the flow. My own story of how I became a spiritual jeweler is an example.

Through a series of suggestions and events, I was guided into making malas and eventually became a spiritual jeweler. A client asked me to make an Amethyst ring for her that a Kabbalist recommended. I phoned him to get the specifics and he decided to teach me how to create jewelry that would bring blessings into people's lives. He explained to me Kabbalah means receiving that universal truth which is behind all belief systems and philosophies. Before I started to work with him, I needed to make sure this really worked.

He determined my Personal Gemstones and I started wearing them. Opportunities started to come my way, and my business blossomed. I found out for myself that it did work so I started to work with him. Within a few months after attending his numerology workshops I had a profound insight—this Universe consists of mathematical equations, and the numbers all have significance and meaning. That night while sleeping, I had a vision. The knowledge was imparted subtly to me, on how to determine which gemstones are just right for a person. The next morning I telephoned the Kabbalist and told him, "I know how to determine Personal Gemstones." He confirmed I had the ability.

I grew into a spiritual jeweler. I never imaged I would be doing what I do today. I was a yoga/meditation teacher since 1974. All I wanted to do was burn off my karma and liberate myself. If you listen to the God in others, listen to your intuition, be in the flow and follow through, you'll be guided into what you should be doing and how you should serve others.

I would like to share with you some concepts that have served me well.

1. **Do what you love, what you are passionate about.** If you do not know what that is yet, "To thy own self be true". Find out who you are, work on yourself spiritually, and you will blossom and manifest your potential.

2. **If you are just starting your business, do something every day towards it.** You may be working for someone else, but you can do one thing each day for your business and eventually it will create a snowball affect. One thing leads to three things to five things till you are asking for flexible hours at work so you can run your business on the side, until the day your business is supporting you.

3. **For the first few years, put the money you make back into your business.** Your business will grow and eventually support you.

4. **Be fair** in your dealings with customers and treat them as you would like to be treated.

5. **Try everything** to see what works for you, but try to do it in an inexpensive manner.

6. **Debt is hard to pay off.** It accumulates. Try not to go into debt. Be thrifty.

7. **Be open to others' input.** Joining an organization like Network for Empowering Woman (NEW) has brought methods, techniques and insights that were not within my scope. You can benefit from networking especially with an uplifting organization like NEW.

8. **Serve the God/Infinity** in your clients with integrity, ethics and wishing them well.

9. **Give.** When you give something without expectation it comes back to you ten-fold.

10. **Overcoming obstacles.** Sometimes when you are doing something great, obstacles will come up. It is like giving birth to a child. When a woman gives birth to a great soul, the labor will be difficult because she is burning off karma and the karma of the child. Go within and draw upon your spirit to rise above for ultimate success.

The deeper the well you tap into, the more success you will have on all levels. Meditate, do yoga, pray, be around your spiritual community and take walks in nature. Hug a tree. Do some selfless service or good deed for others, and do something for your spirit and self-improvement every day. Make the connection with the essence of your soul and infinity will guide you.

When the heart opens and the mind experiences infinity, you see infinity in everything and everyone. To quote William Blake, "To see the world in a grain of sand, and to see heaven in a wild flower, hold infinity in the palm of your hands, and eternity in an hour". Spiritual experiences and being spiritually minded brings consciousness into your life and in managing your business.

The reality is, we are all connected. God and his creation are one. God, that infinite power, is unlimited. Do not limit yourself. True prosperity begins when the heart center opens. It's like creating a love relationship with infinity. The more you go within and resonate and connect with infinity, the more you will attract God, Goods and Goodness.

Stand with your hands in a cup of prayer to receive with an attitude of gratitude. If it resonates with your mind, heart and soul, take action and walk through life wishing everyone well.

RACHEL E. HART, Award-winning Spiritual Jeweler, author of "Mala Meditation for Physical, Mental and Spiritual Prosperity" also determines Personal Gemstones that bring blessings of well-being, prosperity and protection. Rachel also does readings for couples, and determines gemstones that will enhance your life together. Visit www.SacredGems.com to learn more about Rachel's services, read testimonies and see jewelry and malas. Join her monthly online newsletter "Empowering Gemstones" and to request a free catalog call 562-402-3537.

CHAPTER 33

Follow Your Heart

The Only Path To Fulfillment

CHRISTINE KLOSER

HAVE YOU EVER HAD the nagging feeling if you don't change your life drastically, you'll end up living someone else's life, instead of your own? This was the feeling I had in April 1988 when I was about to graduate from college in New England and decided to move three thousand miles away to sunny San Diego. Up until that time, I had always done what was expected of me. I got pretty good grades in school and competed as a figure skater and jazz dancer. Overall I was an agreeable, disciplined young woman. I had been happy with the status quo until I began to think about life after college.

Maybe you've asked yourself some of the same questions I did. What was I going to do for a living? What would make me happy? How would I know if I was doing what I was meant to be doing? What does it take to succeed? Where did I belong?

Perhaps you've had the same desire to follow your heart and design your life not dictated by what society "thinks" you should do. Society wanted me to dress up in a business suit and go to on campus interviews, which I did once and vowed never to do again.

Instead, I listened to my heart, hopped into a tiny VW with two girl-friends, and headed as far away from New England as I could get without having to take a boat!

My willingness to take the first step and go against the "norm" was the moment I knew an incredible journey had begun, and I let my heart guide me through the experiences of life. Have you ever had one of those moments—when life forces you to take a close look inside your heart and soul? Yes, this is when you begin to discover your true answers.

What answers do you hear when you listen to your heart? I can tell you they are not answers rooted in fear, doubt, worry or lack. They are answers anchored in love, possibility, hope, faith, belief and authentic desire. I imagine if you take a moment right now and reflect on your own life, you can identify the first time you followed your heart, or at least the first time you felt your true heart's desire calling you.

I can honestly say my life would never be what it is today if I hadn't made the leap of faith to follow my heart. I moved to San Diego without a job, a place to live and didn't know a single person except the two friends who had moved with me. This decision set me on a path that has led to a more fulfilling life than I ever could have imagined.

What major decisions have you made in life to lead you down your path to fulfillment? Maybe you ended a bad relationship, started a business, discovered your dream job, or quit it all to be a stay-at-home mom? When you begin to reflect on your greatest rewards, you'll discover these decisions probably came from your heart, rather than your head. Your heart is the best place for a decision to come from.

There's a place inside you that knows what is right. For me, it was saying "good-bye" to my family and friends in Connecticut, and saying "hello" to California. The greatest joy of following my heart in 1988 was to know that I could actually do it. I learned I was willing to risk big to win big, and not be afraid of the unknown. Maybe all those years of competitive figure skating and being in front of judges built my confidence and helped me realize I could take a risk, and maybe even fail (and fall), without thinking I was a failure.

The concept of failing, without considering yourself a failure, is one of the key elements needed in order to be confident in following your heart. If you're afraid of failure, you'll never take a chance on your dream. Failure is actually one of the best ways to succeed, because it teaches you what didn't work and brings you one step closer to what will. Take a look at the most successful people you know. Chances are, they followed their heart, took risks, failed several times and simply kept on going. The only failures are people whose dreams get buried with them.

What is the real risk in following your heart? Yes, failure is one risk, but you now know failure is practically necessary if you're going to experience success. Looking like a fool is another risk. What will people think if you follow your heart, try something new and it doesn't work? They may look at you with judgment, disapproval or worry. But people who follow their heart aren't concerned with what other people think.

Contemplate this for a moment. Have you ever not done something because of what others might think? Chances are, like me, you've lived to regret those decisions.

As long as we're eliminating the risks of following your heart, what are some other risks we can dispel? How about this one? "I don't know how." Perhaps you've thought about following your heart, maybe to start a new business, buy your first investment property or start a family, but you feel stressed, overwhelmed and don't know where to begin.

Here's something to think about. Did Thomas Edison know how to make a light bulb when he started? No. Did Alexander Graham Bell know how to make a telephone when he began tinkering around? No. Does anyone know how to do something big right off the bat? Chances are, no.

The point? Don't wait until you "know it all" before you start to fulfill your heart's desire, because chances are, you'll never know enough. Get started on your dreams; trust the Universe to show you and teach you what you need to be successful.

This has been one of the greatest lessons to propel me to success. If I waited until I knew "enough," you certainly wouldn't be holding this book in your hands! When you truly listen and follow your heart and have a clear vision of how you'll serve others, the Universe comes to help you in miraculous ways.

Your heart is like a compass. It knows the way, if you allow it to show you. Be mindful, however, not to abandon your heart's desire when you experience challenges. Your heart knows what you need to become the best possible "you" can ever be, even if it's quite unpleasant at times.

Trust your heart. Ask for its input and how it feels about a decision and then let it guide you. Whatever you dream of is yours for the asking. This is not to say it will be handed to you on a silver platter. But, it will be given to you if you maintain faith and continue to be guided by your true desire. Somehow, miracles will appear, and you will see signs that you are on your right path. Ask yourself, "What is the Universe trying to tell me through my heart? Am I truly open to follow my heart and to learn the lessons I'm meant to learn? Am I open to receive the blessings, too?"

You will reach your destiny as long as you keep moving forward and follow your heart. Be open to learn all you're meant to learn through the good times and the challenges. If you do, you simply can't go wrong.

Your heart truly is your compass; let it point you in the direction of your dreams.

CHRISTINE KLOSER is the Founder of NEW Entrepreneurs, Inc. An entrepreneur since 1991, Christine has helped thousands of women take charge of their personal, financial, spiritual and business lives. She has appeared on numerous radio and TV shows, and hosts her own television program in Los Angeles. Christine is also a member of the Who's Who of Empowering Executives and Professionals, and a sought after coach and speaker. You can reach her at 310.745.0794 or www.newentrepreneurs.com.

⌒

CHAPTER 34

Coming FULL-Circle Into Your Ideal Life

Using Circle Principles To Bring Success, Balance & Magic Into Your Life

DEBORAH KOPPEL MITCHELL

When women come together in circle with clear intent and presence, something very magical and powerful occurs. There is a synergy created in circle, a presence that is healing and indescribable in full by words . . .

AS A WOMAN AND AN ENTREPRENEUR, I have found maintaining balance in my life to be my biggest challenge. My own health, both physical and spiritual, has seemed to be the first thing on my long "To Do" list I let slip. Every Life Coach and book on success conveys a strong message of the importance of creating a spiritual practice to be included in our daily routine. Being an entrepreneur can also be very isolating. As busy as we all are in our lives, connecting and sharing with one another can be the key to creating a successful, healthful and balanced life. With the little time I do have to spend with others, "authentic connection" has become the utmost priority. Coming together in circle with others of like mind, has become a way to fill myself up spiritually, which in turn positively impacts all areas of my life.

I was inspired to create my first women's circle at a time when besides having a wonderful core of women friends, I was meeting one incredible woman after another. I couldn't help but feel that bringing us all together under the same roof at the same time would create magic. I was so right, and the desire to come together with other like-minded women was strong. This continues to this day.

A *Circle* can be defined as when two or more come together in the space of a circle to listen and be heard while being fully present. Whether it is a sewing circle, book, bible study, an investment or spirituality group, or a simple gathering— there is a synergy created in the container of a circle. Here, magic and unconditional love is tangible.

There has been a growing number of books and other resources supporting what has now become the "Women's Circles Movement," an extension of what has been called "The Women's Spirituality Movement," a kind of *Evolved Feminism* for the New Millennium.

It has been said the forming of circles creates a ripple effect. . . Each woman who is a part of a circle carries the positive energy of the experience of that circle out into her world of relationships, which continues to expand out into the world, the universe, and All That Is! This same concept is also brought out in Dr. Jean Shinoda Bolen's book *The Millionth Circle*. There is recognition of the great impact this quality of connecting and pure intention can have on us as individuals and in our world.

In the book, *Women Circling the Earth*, author Beverly Engel, shares ways to "join the circle and begin making significant changes in your family, in your community and in the world." They include:

- Creating or joining a circle
- Widening the circle by bringing circle principles into other aspects of your life
- Conducting your life according to circle principles
- Dedicating your energy and resources to organizations and causes that advocate circle principles

Two circle principles that are the most positive and powerful are those of being present and willing. Whether or not you choose to be part of a women's circle, it serves us all to be aware of the positive effects of being willing to be present and open in our lives.

There is a common thread connecting us that becomes obvious when we experience the sharing taking place in a circle. Whether it is desire for success, personal development, or the ideal relationship, we are all basically striving to experience purpose, love with one another and love of Self. Now more than ever, heart connections and acknowledging our connection to each other, is paramount.

Like many of you, I have been examining and redefining my perspective and many life roles as a woman, life partner and human being. Old ways of thinking no longer work at this point, and ideas about traditional gender roles and views on success have changed. I find a growing awareness of how my attitude has been shifting to a much deeper place.

Choosing our focus more on creating balance and harmony while contributing to life as a whole has taken the forefront. Beyond counting my blessings, I now focus on simply filling my heart with appreciation. This brings me to a more receptive state of being. Therefore, I have more to give and in-turn I receive so much more for which to be grateful. It all comes full circle.

I am also consciously not pushing so hard at what anyone else, including myself, have perceived as a successful life. My lesson has been to ease up on myself and simply live in love, compassion, presence and ease. These are some of the gifts I have experienced due to my participation in circles. Each of these can be applied to our every day lives.

CIRCLE PRINCIPLES TO CREATE HARMONIOUS, FULLFILLING LIVES

- Create a "Ritual" before jumping into your daily activities. For example: light a candle and take time to pause to center yourself—to simply connect and be in a state of appreciation

- Guide your gatherings into a "single conversation" with one person speaking at a time, while all others are listening and fully present with one another
- Take time to slow down and connect with one another and the ONENESS. . . in silence
- Mutually support one another
- Breathe deeply, filling yourself up with love and appreciation in every moment
- And finally, (the one I find most challenging) have absolutely no judgment towards others and yourself

Taking part in circle gatherings brings authenticity into our lives and has a healing effect on the world. We are reminded that we were born with magnificent wisdom and a divine nature. Being in circle can serve as an important reminder to each of us to tap into that "Goddess" part of us, and not get lost or caught up in the hectic pace we have created in our lives.

Living in the present with the attitude that ALL is right, right NOW, can have a powerful impact on every aspect of our lives. This creates flow, and facilitates the letting go of all our preconceived ideas of the way we think our lives and selves are supposed to be. The gift is that of grace in your life and all around you.

As women, we can reflect the powerful yet subtle force symbolized by the Statue of Liberty. . .

"We can choose to be willing to take on the strength and attitude of that of a 'Goddess Warrior,' strong, Feminine Energy. The 'Goddess Warrior' does not have to use weapons and go to battle physically. It is more that they use their mind, their consciousness, their belief systems, to move the world. . . "

—From Cynthia Brown's *The Wild Women's Path*™ article series in *Spheres Women's Circles* magazine.

I am now able to see that creating and being part of a women's circle has been a reflection of my acceptance of my own femininity. As I have embraced these incredible women in my life, I have embraced my Self. This experience is one of tremendous healing and continues to positively affect every area of my life.

DEBORAH KOPPEL MITCHELL is a Circle Leader and the publisher of Spheres Women's Circles magazine and web site. Drawing on more than 10 years of experience in marketing, public relations, and events, her work continues to evolve as she creates more venues for connecting with the intention of benefiting all. Deborah resides in Pacific Palisades, CA, with her husband. She is available for speaking, consultations, and to assist in creating circles. Phone: (310) 230-0032 | Email: spherescircles@earthlink.net | Visit: www.sphereswomenscircles.com.

CHAPTER 35

There Are Miracles Everywhere

ALICE ASPEN MARCH

WHEN I MOVED FROM MICHIGAN to California 40 years ago, I didn't even know what a miracle was. I had a sense my life could be better, would be better, and that I had to move.

Today, I look back to see how many portals I had to go through, how much learning I had to do, and how courageous I was. I am forever grateful I took the first step to live without knowing all the answers, to go against the culture, to live in the question. This sounds like a credo for everyone who wants to find happiness and success.

Miracles are my personal messages from the Universe. They play important roles in our lives and have shown me five vital truths to live by:

- Pay careful attention to the synchronicities in your life
- Live in the moment
- Tell yourself the truth
- Take yourself seriously
- Develop your intuitive self to make the invisible visible.

My work, The Attention Factor®, grew out of an awful family crisis which I now view as a life evolving gift. I discovered my youngest son's drug abuse when he was 11. Terrified I might lose him, I went searching for the role I played in his self-destructive behavior. Along the way, I had an epiphany.

Another word for epiphany is miracle, especially when it gives the answer we're seeking. Through this miracle/epiphany, I developed a new paradigm for living, which led to my son's recovery and finding my life's work. The Attention Factor® is a system I have designed to support people's consciousness of getting, giving and handling the attention they get and giving others what they need/want for healthy living.

Recently over a Christmas break, my husband and I traveled by ship around New Zealand. I chose to stay in a port city, to hang out, perhaps meet a new friend instead of taking another nature excursion with my fellow passengers.

My choice totally changed the direction of my life. While roaming through the local shopping center, I went inside one of the shops and Anne, the saleswoman, approached me, backed away, started to cry and asked if I was a healer. I answered, "yes", and asked how she knew; she replied she could feel it in my energy field. We decided to stay connected through e-mails. Three months later, Anne took an unexpected trip to Canada and had a nine-hour stopover in Los Angeles. I picked her up at the airport, and we spent six hours walking, talking, and eating together. Before she left, she generously asked what she could do for me. I answered that I would like to return to New Zealand to work.

We planned a fall trip. When one airline didn't have space for me, I asked the sales person for help. I ended up using accumulated airline miles and spent a total of $ 14.98 to fly round-trip Business Class. A financial miracle, surely.

When a childhood friend in Canada heard where I was going, he suggested I e-mail a mutual friend in Michigan who was also planning a trip there. We discovered we would be in the same city at the same time, and made arrangements to meet. As miracles will have it, we bumped into each other the night before we planned.

My old friends were with their tour director, Mark, who asked us to join their table. Mark proceeded to amaze us as he began to finish my sentences. He told me he had the special network I needed in Auckland, and I must meet several people, including his mother. I was almost dumbfounded. The miracles were multiplying!

I changed my plans and called everyone on Mark's list. His mother and I had a life changing breakfast together, because she suggested I call a group called Zenergy—facilitators who were working for social change. She shared how her son Mark had inherited his Irish grandmother's psychic gifts and had "read" me.

The day before I left, I had tea with the Zenergy group. We exchanged workbooks and discovered we had done identical work! I recognized while I had been creating workshops, giving keynote addresses, and writing, I was really a natural facilitator. I felt as if I had "docked!" Mark attended my Auckland workshop, and told everyone there I must continue to speak out about the power of attention.

Returning from New Zealand, I located others who were doing facilitation work. I have become a Partner in an international group called Appreciative Inquiry Consulting, L.L.C. to collaborate, contribute and spread my work on a grander, wider level.

In reflecting back over my journey, I've created two personal review questions which are essential. Ask yourself:

- Where do you get the passion and the energy to continue to create, even when the going gets tough and other parts of your life conspire to invade your life?
- Have you learned the art of starting over, of finding gracious, compassionate listeners, of letting go of personally toxic people and situations?

Your energy, your inventiveness and your spirit will grow when you can know the answers and can honestly answer "Yes!"

Stumbling upon how to balance our lives in the various roles we play has been my biggest miracle to date; it has contributed greatly to my son's healing. Everyone needs distinctive kinds of attention. The kind of attention you surround yourself with is the root cause of your feelings, your behavior and your success.

In order to thrive, you have to know how to care for yourself, how to nurture and nourish yourself, when and how to ask for support and from whom. You continually need to ask yourself:

- Are you in charge of your feelings or do you wait for others to do things to make you feel a certain way?
- Who is coming into your life and how do you feel with them?
- Are you comfortable, excited, feeling included, feeling supported, feeling honored?

Your feelings drive your passions and your energy to keep doing what you're doing. It takes practice to identify your feelings and to own them.

As you choose to become what your miracles call you to, you need sufficient faith to take risks. You need vision, the strength and fortitude to work alone and often on the cutting edge.

I've spent many years cleaning out old habits and beliefs, so I would have clearer vision and a greater connection to my intuition. The kind of attention we receive in our childhood lives with us forever. We have to re-work both our emotional and physical wiring. This is a process involving time, patience and sometimes just being still. It takes both parts of us to recognize miracles. Sometimes we feel them, and other times we see them.

Years ago, millions read Jean Auel's enthralling book *The Clan of the Cave Bear*. Her main character is a pre-historic woman who discovers her life's path through finding her "totems" that only she could see. Perhaps the reason Auel's book was a bestseller for so long is because it introduced us to the spiritual guidance we receive along our way when we are awake, aware and present enough to recognize Universal direction.

Give yourself a special gift; do whatever it takes to answer positively to these final three questions:

- Do you take the time to observe the totems in your life?
- Do you respect and listen to your inner self?
- Do you trust yourself enough to know and to ask for the kind of attention you need?

Experience has shown me a resounding "Yes!" supplies the clarity you need to attract a success-filled, supported and passionate life journey.

ALICE ASPEN MARCH, has spent twenty-five years researching peoples' needs for healthy, successful living. As an expert on the effects of television viewing, she created "Latch-Key Kids", Emmy nominated Documentary and was appointed by the California State Senate to the White House Conference on the Family. Hundreds of people worldwide have acknowledged the difference her work on attention has meant in their lives through her speeches, seminars and coaching. She can be reached directly at 310.476.2084 or at her website www.theattentionfactor.com .

⌒

CHAPTER 36

Listening To Your Spirit

Accepting Guidance From Within

CINDI PRINGLE

BECOMING CLEAR on your heart's desire, through which your spirit is speaking, and then acting upon it can be a struggle throughout your lifetime. You are bombarded with so many external influences—from your family of origin and educational processes to economic circumstances and societal trends—that it's a challenge to make choices that truly resonate with who you are.

You can train yourself, however, to minimize the effect of external messages on your decision-making and listen more intently to your internal voice. Introverts, who comprise only 25 percent of the U.S. population, will find this easier than extroverts, who typically are energized by others and, thus, may be more prone to the distraction of external influences. If you don't know where you fall on the introvert-extrovert scale, a quick measure is available through the temperament test in the book, *Please Understand Me*, by David Keirsey.

No matter what your temperament is, as a woman you likely will find focus on the self does not come easily. As the gender genetically programmed to nurture, women often place care of the self, as opposed to others, last in their priorities or—worse yet—they neglect themselves emotionally, physically and spiritually. Taking care of yourself takes practice—the first step comes with acceptance that your needs are not going to be met entirely through others. You may not even realize deep within you, a desire to be taken care of or "parented" exists—a holdover expectation from childhood, especially if your upbringing left emotional scars from neglect or abandonment. Release yourself from the entrapment of the child-victim, yearning for fulfillment from those who have been unable to meet your needs, and empower yourself to tend to your heart's desire.

Remember, you came into this world alone, as a spirit born into flesh for a brief time, and you will leave this world alone as well. In the time that you are alive, you will meet many people and connect with a few. Those who are in your "inner circle" will be the most important to your journey of self-realization and fulfillment. Your relationships with others will teach you how to be in an interaction with another person and to remain true to yourself, how to collaborate and compromise, and how to let go when a relationship is not serving you.

Creating and maintaining healthy boundaries in relation to others will serve you well in business, particularly if your venture involves family members or friends as partners. Launching a business relationship with those with whom you have had other previous interactions can facilitate collaboration because you already know one another. At the same time it can complicate a working agreement because the new relationship likely will require new "rules of engagement." All relationships that develop beyond mere acquaintances eventually present power conflicts that must be negotiated and resolved. Therefore, a business partnership that overlaps a pre-existing personal or professional relationship most certainly will involve a new set of negotiations that lead to compromise and collaboration.

You will be in a better position to negotiate on your own behalf if you have spent time getting to know yourself. If introspection is an uncommon experience for you, you may take steps toward refining this process by learning to meditate, practicing yoga or some form of exercise followed by relaxation, journaling and writing down dreams when you wake up, seeking counsel or taking classes that lead to self exploration. Be gentle with yourself and know the discovery of self is a lifelong process—it is the journey of the soul and the purpose for human life on Earth.

Once you become attuned to your inner voice, you'll begin to notice patterns in your life, including choices you've made, similarities among people you've been close to, and what constitutes painful and joyful memories. Though you may feel you'd rather forget than remember, you can find clarity in what your life has revealed to you so far. You are these patterns and although you may make different choices from now on, your acceptance of all of the experiences that make you who you are today will accelerate your growth into the person you want to become.

Learning to distinguish between circumstances that are beyond your control from those you're empowered to choose among will help you become emotionally reinforced for the occasions when the right choices for you aren't very clear. Ultimately the choice may be to "let go and let God," or whatever Higher Power you put your faith in, to do the work in your life. For those of us who have lived with abundance all of our lives, this may be a particularly difficult task because we have the sense that life is and always has been within our control. It is the wise woman who embraces the truth in the adage, "There, but for the grace of God, go I," and understands that life can change at any moment—for better or worse. You may feel a sense of relief in the act of surrendering to the fact that your destiny is a combination of your free will and some form of determinism, whether you believe that emanates from a contract with God or some other spiritual guidance.

No matter what your faith, you inevitably hold dear certain values and beliefs. Determine what those are and then infuse them into your business. If you like to make people happy, perhaps this becomes the "mission statement" that drives your business. Know your intentions are powerful—your thoughts, put into motion, become action. Make sure your motives are pure and authentic. If you are acting to avenge yourself or to "hurt" a competitor by some manipulative deed, you are behaving negatively. There is a growing body of evidence, particularly in medical literature, that negative thoughts can have reciprocal effects, e.g. the person who puts negativity into motion will suffer the deleterious effects as well.

Take a regular and fierce moral inventory of yourself; are you acting with integrity and courage at all times? If you see something an employee or co-worker is doing that seems wrong, confront it as soon as you have enough information to speak accurately about the situation. Women often tend to avoid conflict and confrontation, so override this tendency as quickly as you can. Summon your courage, especially if you are the manager—the staff wants to know someone is in charge and minding the shop. They will resent a supervisor who does not "earn her keep" by making sure the rules are observed.

Courage will be the character trait you'll have to call on frequently when starting your own business. As you scan the environment to determine whether you have a reasonable chance of success with your venture, there will come a time when you'll simply have to feel the fear and do it anyway. Look at it like jumping off the high dive and hoping you land comfortably in the water—knowing there's no guarantee the plunge you take will make the splash you hope for.

If, in the process of coming to know yourself, you've developed a strong internal voice or intuition, you may be able to recognize indications that your plans have little chance for reaching fruition.

As the Buddhists counsel: Do not persist if there is significant resistance. There may be forces working against you of which you are unaware; at some point, an accounting of all the factors that stand in the way of an idea may lead you to the healthy decision not to proceed.

It takes courage to let go of a dream, just as it does to conceive one. American women, in particular, have been acculturated in a society geared toward achievement and success; their feelings of shame emanating from their perception of failure need to be acknowledged and processed. However, if you believe that no experience is lived without some benefit, then you will seek the wisdom and truth left behind which you can apply to your next undertaking.

Whether your venture succeeds or not, be sure to credit all of those who helped in the process. Celebrate all of the parts that make the whole. Acknowledge your involvement is but a fraction of the outcome. You never know where or when you will interact with these people again.

CINDI feels fortunate that her first-grade teacher's insightfulness about her potential to be a published author, after she wrote a story about a cow that always did what it was supposed to, also turned out to be the career that would fuel her soul. A self-described storyteller, Cindi has been presenting information in print, on radio and television and via the Internet, among other venues, as a career journalist for more than 20 years. www.tellyourstory.tv

CHAPTER 37

As You Wish, So It Is So

WENDY ROBBINS

I HAVE A DREAM—that one day we'll all live as genies on Earth. I know the "unspoken till now" secrets of the genies. Want to know what I know? Ok, but it's only being revealed because you are pinky-swearing that you are forever changed from this moment on, just by reading a simple story with all the life/love lessons a human genie will ever need to make all her/his dreams real.

You are saying "bye" to 'circus-stances' and "hello" to 'free-ality.' What do I mean by that? Our lives mimicking a 3-ring circus will not entertain us unless we are the ringmasters. We are the participant not the spectator. Our act is to be powerful, passionate, free, and real hence the name Free-ality.

It sounds amazingly death defying, life affirming, tell me more now, doesn't it? Ok, I ask only a couple of things from you, and in exchange your wishes will come true! Fair? Duh. Ok, I want you to be open to wonder—to read as a child—full of imagination and delight—sure, BE really juicy and delicious right now. See with your eyes closed. Taste with your fingertips. Get it? This story doesn't ask you to be ordinary—it recognizes that unarmored place within you that is all about the "yes to life." So in your yes— here's the story that guarantees all your wishes will come true. Wahoo!!!

Start by saying out loud, "I believe that my wishes will come true. I believe. I believe." If you don't—don't read on. By the way what do you wish for? Take a moment right now, and come up with something that inspires you. Do you have goose bumps? See cause, this is a tale for believers; in faith and trust our tale unfolds—yes, life is but a dream . . .

Genies used to live in the Soul-ar—(it's a play on words) soular system of "I Can't," in the land of Limitations—then there was a revolt away from the darkness and an awakening into the Light. It is in this place I first met my genie friend and this is the summa- rized instruction she shared that changed my life.

1. **Genies know what they want, and why they want it.** They don't worry about the how. They trust that their dreams will come true. They don't take themselves too seriously. It would- n't make sense not to believe in their wishes coming true. They understand that they're perfect as they are and that they can easily tap into abundance. They don't listen to the little voice that complains and lies to them saying their wishes won't come true. They think that voice is funny and simply a consideration that they choose to consider not real. They know that the little voice inside is from the dark side—from limitations, lack, and scarcity and for protection and guidance; they pray and acknowledge:

2. **"Bestowers of bliss, keepers of the flame ignite the passion within all hearts. . . we are slivers of the One source that cre- ates all.** We're a drop of water that makes up the ocean. The stuff stars are made of. The vibration that is a child's lullaby. Part of the interconnecting web of all life that is connected to

the heart of the Creator of all." Genies wishes are always for the good of all. They are about serving others—because of that intention and commitment they always easily attract what they want. Like attracts like—that's a universal law.

3. **Genies love silence.** That's why they only say—"As you wish!" and "It is so." They especially love the silence between words. It's not hard or complicated; only thinking makes it so. This creation process is just about focused clarity, intention, passion, intuition, commitment, unstopability, and faith. Notice there is no thinking in the recipe.

4. **Being.** "They take time in silence to envision easily birthing a wish. They know who to BE to activate the wish. They know wishes don't come true just by "doing," but rather by Being the change they want to see in the world. Genies and humans give form to the formless by simply and joyfully being a sculptor of matter and light, which makes the invisible, visible.

5. **Peace.** Sometimes, the "work of art" called life isn't always a "master peace" - we are sometimes unclear, unspecific, unfocused, so we draw in a dysfunctional relationship, a lawsuit, illness, lack of money, happiness, love, and health—whatever. These become lessons for us to transform fear into love, anger into compassion, rage into forgiveness. . . and finally mastering peace is possible.

6. **All the events or experiences or circus-stances are neutral.** Humans often unconsciously react to things going on in their lives based on stories they make up about things. Humans make meaning out of everything. Genies don't. They look at everything as neutral and rarely make up stories that limit them. They know that they are co-creating free-ality—so all of creation is limitless. They know that everything is a play of consciousness. So they relax, step back, and witness and respond so that they are always whole, in love, learning and

shifting. It's all part of the game/dream called life. They think life is a verb, and like water, fleeting, while humans think life is a noun and a rock. So humans become rigid, stuck, and unable to shift. . .

7. **Fearlessness.** Here's the part of the story that calls for us not to be attached to how the lessons are packaged because they all have gifts for us. Genies love these gifts. They never think, "I'm too powerful, I'm scared to manifest, or I'd better be careful for what I wish for because it may come true, and then what would I do?" Humans get scared to create what they want and often times sabotage their power and "genie ability." Humans are often fearful of their greatness.

8. **Humans' brains are made up of 85% water and hold the amount of information equivalent to what is contained in 20 million books.** 20 million books in your head. The way to get to the field that knows everything is to be quiet, with no distractions, no strategies, no tactics, no drama, nothing. Just quiet.

9. **Trust the spirit living inside you that has read the 20 million books will speak to the spirit who wrote an infinite number of books and knows all, and you will simply be in conversation.** Then all you need to do is stay open and listen. That's your part of the conversation—pay rapt attention without your censoring filters on.

10. **In this state of quiet, where you are listening as though they were spirit's last cherished words, you visualize who you are going to be, and what you are going to have and do.** Just notice. Genies often dance, frolic, or wave a magic wand as they eat something yummy so they can listen, touch, move, taste and see the invisible become visible. It's real before it is. The more engaged they are with all their senses, the faster it appears. They experience it into creation. Humans tend to get

stressed, desiring, desperate, wanting, come from lack, thinking it has to be a certain way, fearful of the consequences of having or not having the particular wish, focused on the "future" which is all made up in the present. Genies are just focused on the joy of the present.

11. **In the present, you live in the land where promises are kept and possibilities are born, and from this space where the air hums and smells of gardenias and jasmine—in your stillness and inner knowing you are a walking, listening, talking temple of ecstasy, you create and master peace.** You see yourself in creation—having your wishes come true easily. This is your daily practice.

12. **You will see exactly how you did it.** You will experience the exact steps you took to manifest the formless into specific form. You now actually write out the blueprint for your life design. You choose to be the architect of intention and commitment; this is your strong foundation.

13. **Then party down.** Genies love and live to celebrate. Gratitude and joy are the characteristics that ensure dreams will come true. Love the child within—this is her/his part of the recipe— it's licking the scrumptious hu/manifestation dough, the laughter, dancing, painting, poetry, spinning, sculpting light, jumping on beds, making cookies, blowing bubbles, getting massages, pampering, a weekend getaway. You are in such faith that your intention is clear and done, you're literally out of your mind in delight. Without the celebration, your wishes may come true but it will take longer and won't be nearly as much fun or filled with wonder and delight, so what's the point? Have fun!!! Your wish has been granted, as you wished! So it is so!

WENDY ROBBINS attended the Julliard School as an actor, directed/wrote/produced documentary films for 13 years and won 2 Emmy's. She co-invented "The Tingler" head massager with no previous experience. Thanks to a perfect business partner, she started with $10k of debt and made millions within 2 years! She makes dreams real with a series of life transforming CD's and 31-day systems that blow hearts and minds open. She can be reached directly at wendy@everythingforlove.com or 310 288 1519 or visit online at www.nowheretomillionaire.com and www.everythingforlove.com

⌒

CHAPTER 38

Dancing On The Wheel Of Life

Balance Business & Family,
Body & Mind, Heart & Soul

BARBARA SCHIFFMAN

"A successful life can be like a successful tightrope-walk" accord-ing to "Life 101" author Peter McWilliams. "Sometimes the balance pole dips violently one way, sometimes it dips gently the other, and sometimes it's perfectly still."

DOES YOUR LIFE feel like you're edging slowly forward on a tightrope, clutching your balance pole so you won't slip off?

In our busy 21st century lives, we have more opportunities to pursue, more information to process, and more choices to make than ever before. If you have a family, career and/or business to manage, friends and loved ones who need you, plus dreams and goals to achieve, it's hard to feel as if your life is in balance more than an inch at a time.

CREATING HARMONY & MAINTAINING BALANCE

The dictionary defines balance as "harmony of design" and "maintaining equilibrium." I define Life Balance as sensing and being aware that each part of my life is distinct yet interconnected. It's also having the ability to stay centered and to bounce back quickly when events and/or people throw me off-center. To maintain equilibrium, I envision myself dancing in the center of my unique Wheel of Life with gratitude, connectedness and joy.

What are the spokes on your Wheel of Life—the distinctive yet connected facets of your Life-Circle?

Lakota Indians believe everything the Creator does is in a circle. The most feminine symbol in the universe is the spiral, which is an upward-moving circle. Even the cycles of Grandmother Moon flow in a circle from New Moon to Full Moon and back again. Since the Moon influences our reproductive and emotional cycles, it's no wonder many women synchronize with the Moon's phases.

RITUALIZING CIRCLES, SPIRALS & CYCLES

So how can you use ancient Life-Cycle symbols to maintain equilibrium in today's busy world?

One way is to pay attention to the Moon's phases to better tune into your own life-rhythms. Many women participate in New or Full Moon ceremonies, alone or with friends. They pause for a few hours each month to honor the cycles of their busy lives. Since I began doing this eight years ago, I've gained a stronger connection with whatever is going on in my life each month. When I stop to appreciate my life, I can feel it evolving.

During New or Full Moon ceremonies, I reflect on the things, events and people from the past month for which I'm grateful. Some months I'm just grateful for surviving it! I also ask for energetic help with projects and personal changes in the coming month from the spiritual energies working within and around me. I'm always amazed at how expressing gratitude and asking for help at the New and/or Full Moon allows energetic support to show up as if by magic!

TUNING INTO NATURAL RHYTHMS & SEASONS

Two books I highly recommend about Moon Rituals which will help you create your own Balance Ceremonies are: Jan Spiller's "New Moon Astrology" (Bantam Books) and Diane Stein's "Casting the Circle: A Woman's Book of Ritual" (The Crossing Press). Jan includes affirmations that resonate with Astrology's 12 Zodiac signs to be written down when the New Moon is in the corresponding sign. Diane shares rituals for each Moon phase plus the year's growing seasons and other sun/moon balance-points.

The seasons and other sun/moon balance-points were honored in Celtic ceremonies to mark the beginnings of spring, summer, autumn and winter. Tuning into the Earth's natural rhythm gives us a sense of how we "plant seeds" in our own life (spring), how they grow (summer), how we harvest them (autumn) and how we replenish our energy (winter). Taking time out for renewal is essential for today's women to recharge our energy and prepare for new projects, cycles and relationships.

Another way to connect with the cycles of our lives is by energizing the Four Elements within and around us. The Four Elements resonate with Earth (our body and tangible world), Air (mental processes such as visioning, analyzing and communicating), Water (our emotional flow and relationships) and Fire (our spiritual and intuitive connections). I take one "baby step" each month for each Life Element to stimulate and increase its positive energy in my life.

LIVING "THE BUTTERFLY EFFECT"

By taking small actions, which resonate with physical, mental, emotional and spiritual facets of life, I am consciously practicing Quantum Physics' core-concept known as The Butterfly Effect. This basic principle of both Quantum Physics and Metaphysics is about how small actions create huge energy shifts. It was proven scientifically by a computer experiment in which small wind condition shifts—as gentle as a butterfly's wings—altered weather patterns and created powerful storms half a world away.

So the effect of one small action does increase in energy as it evolves. Also, taking one small action helps clarify the next action to be taken. You don't need to know each step to begin a big journey, since the path will naturally unfold as you proceed.

DANCING AT THE WHEEL'S HUB

Another way circles resonate with spiritual and tangible energy is seen in Astrology's Horoscope Wheel. I use it to evaluate every part of my life and inspire small actions for each, one at a time. The Horoscope is a perfect Wheel of Life, as its 12 spokes each resonate energetically with one "Slice" of Life. Where the spokes intersect at the Wheel's hub creates the center on which we can dance our way through life.

In brief, the Horoscope's "slices" (or Houses) are: 1) Aries = our self-image and how things begin; 2) Taurus = our talents and resources (including income); 3) Gemini = how and what we communicate; 4) Cancer = our home and office environments, our birth-family and how things end; 5) Leo = how we express creativity and love; 6) Virgo = how we contribute to others and heal ourselves; 7) Libra = how we relate to others in committed relationships (especially marriage or business partnerships); 8) Scorpio = how we transform and merge our resources with others (including sexual energy); 9) Sagittarius = how we learn and connect to spiritual paths; 10) Capricorn = our life's calling (career) and how we receive recognition; 11) Aquarius = our life goals and how we relate to groups (including all of humanity); and 12) Pisces = our private lives, dreams and fears.

Within this Wheel, everything in life is connected energetically. I believe taking conscious actions to increase positive energy, or unstick stagnant energy, in each section of the Horoscope helps us gain a deeper sense of connectedness between them all.

We also learn how our lives are not just about our businesses, our families or our health—even when these areas demand most of our attention. By giving every part of life a little bit of attention over a brief period of time, it's no wonder Balance naturally occurs.

Also, the more positive energy we receive and give to others, the higher our personal vibrations rise. Then we automatically add positive energy to the rest of the world through everyone we touch.

By increasing our positive energy in whatever ways suit us—as a sacred mission—we have an incredible opportunity to balance our individual lives, as well as the whole world, from the inside out. What better way could we joyfully live our lives, conduct our business and enjoy our relationships than by Dancing on the Wheel of Life for the benefit of us all?

BARBARA SCHIFFMAN is a Life Balance Coach, Certified Voyager Tarot Coach/Teacher and Inner Guide Meditation Teacher. She assists spiritual entrepreneurs and creatives to energize and evolve their lives. Barbara's EvoLuminus Coaching programs blend Quantum Physics with Energy-Astrology, Archetypal Tarot and Personal Feng Shui in telecourses, private sessions and workshops. Her book series "Dancing on the Wheel of Life" is based on her telecourses. Contact her at 818-848-9040, 800-306-8290, by e-mail at EvoLuminus@yahoo.com or visit www.bschiffman.com.

CHAPTER 39

Parenting From Both Sides Of The Brain

Combining Psychology, Spirituality & Energy Medicine

ADELAIDE SMITH

PARENTING IS A SACRED MISSION. When you become a parent, you are entrusted with the welfare of another human being. Parenting, properly accomplished, is an incredibly difficult job with the potential for being both rewarding and transforming. To "inspire" is to breathe new life into someone. The doctor inspires literally by slapping the newborn on his/her buttocks to initiate a first breath. You, the parent, have the opportunity to inspire your child figuratively through every one of your interactions over a period of many years.

The objective of this chapter is to help you make the most of this opportunity to be an effective parent, and turn every inspiration into a focused and unified realization of your dreams for your child or children. You have all the tools for this task; although some may be rusty or broken, some untouched or lost, and some you may not know you have or are uncertain as to their use. We will explore these tools and discuss how and when to employ them to make you the parent you want to be.

Parenting is a "hands-on" operation. And what kind of hands-on depends on whose hands. No two parents are alike just as no two children are alike. So how does one find the information that will speak to your particular mix of parent and child? For example, are you more comfortable punishing a child for breaking rules or setting up a reward for the child to earn by learning to follow the rules? This choice is complicated by the fact that not only do you have to know what works for you, you have to know what works for the child, and find ways to achieve consistent and positive results for both of you.

Scientists have recognized that one side of the human brain is intuitive while the other is logical. The intuitive brain draws on a core of inner knowing to form opinions and attitudes which hold a strong influence over actions. The logical brain collects information, sorts it, puts it together and gives us a template for action based on facts. Another way of looking at this is the logical brain is "doing" while the intuitive brain is "being". Most of our doing comes from an analysis of facts leading to a perceived logical decision or action. Most of our being comes from seeing ourselves honestly and being comfortable with ourselves as feeling and caring individuals. When we can "Be"our "Doing" is informed by a deeper knowing.

Both the intuitive and logical brains collectively determine our actions in response to any given situation. In order to bring dreams for your children to fruition, there must be a balance between the intuitive and the logical. Achieving this balance on a day-to-day basis, through countless interactions, is a demanding task that can be made easier with a few seemingly simple tools. While these will be introduced in this chapter, each constitutes an area for further reading and study, and there are many resources available for this purpose.

These tools may be classified as either physiological or spiritual, but there is an interaction between the two. Of the physiological tools, the most important is proper breathing. Taking deep, cleansing breaths from the diaphragm muscle just above the belly is essential not only for providing plenty of oxygen to your brain but for maintaining your composure or being "grounded." I give the following instructions to parents and children to help them learn to breathe from the belly:

Put your hands on your lower abdomen. Don't lift your shoulders as you breathe in through your nose. Your hands will rise on your abdomen as your lower lungs fill with air. Then press gently with your hands as you expel the air slowly out of your mouth.

Drinking enough water—not coffee, tea, or soda—is also important to properly hydrate the brain for maximum efficiency. And it is important to choose wisely the type of foods we eat to ensure adequate nourishment of our so-called gray matter. Oxygen, water, and a proper diet promote a healthy body and facilitate a healthy state of mind.

Of the spiritual tools, your connection to Spirit or a Higher Power is paramount. You must know what belief nurtures your soul, your core, or whatever you call that part of you that makes you unique. Closely allied with this is having a system for understanding and appreciating differences between ourselves and others. For instance, suppose your child is frightened by something you perceive as irrational. Rather than a right-brain reflex response ("That's ridiculous, there's nothing to be afraid of."), you will react from a more balanced place of understanding. This will enable you to share your knowledge with the child, and then reinforce this by walking the child through a process to dispel the fear.

A well-known example of a system for understanding differences between and among people is the Enneagram. When I teach parents how to use the Enneagram, they learn that energy follows attention. In the above child-parent example, the child perceived danger when there was none. I point out to the parent that the child automatically pays attention to the possibility of danger, and, would there be anger or shame if the perceived danger were a car accident? With new knowledge, the parent can respond compassionately without anger or shame. Instead, the parent is better able to help the child learn to differentiate between real and imagined dangers.

Less understood among the spiritual tools is the concept of energy flow within the body. Energy flow is, simply put, the electrical current that carries messages between the cells in our body. Negative emotions can create blockage in the system. Our understanding of this can make it a vital building block in maintaining a balanced existence. With further study, some exercises, and a better appreciation of this demonstrable phenomenon; you can cut loose the autopilot, which often blocks energy, and release the energy to flow appropriately throughout your body.

Balance in the context of this chapter does not mean giving up who you are. It means having the ability to choose how you interact with your children instead of merely having a knee-jerk reaction, (reacting to each and every situation as it occurs). When grounded, we can maintain our composure in the face of the unexpected. . . and parenting has lots of the unexpected. Being grounded means you are in control and not letting the ingrained feelings of your intuitive brain or the cold logic of your logical brain take over. It means that you can make better decisions and take actions you will have no cause to regret once the heat of the moment has passed. It helps you make the transition from being a good parent to being a great parent.

I hope this chapter has inspired you as well as given you some valuable information on maintaining balance through being grounded in your parental role. The interactive combination of physiological and spiritual tools provided herein can make a difference in your parenting, your life and the life of your child.

There is, however a caveat: these tools atrophy like muscles if they are recognized but aren't used. Research has shown that repetition is the key in creating physiological "pathways" in the brain, and this same principle applies to building and maintaining your skills as a parent. Using the tools we all possess can and will help you achieve your dreams.

ADELAIDE is a Boston Area Family Therapist specializing in helping parents create their ideal relationship with their children. A passionate student, she has studied psychological, spiritual, and energetic approaches to healing. Colleagues, clients and friends recognize her as a skilled teacher who is able to facilitate growth with humor and compassion. She can be reached at asmith@parentinglifeline.com

CHAPTER 40

⌒

The Path To Personal Resiliency

Learning To Take The Next Bold Step

KATHRYN TULL

SOMETIMES OUR PERSONAL JOURNEY unfolds in a way we never imagined. This turned out to be true for me, and in 1999 I hit a personal low, lower than I knew low could ever go. I found myself at the bottom of an unbelievable nightmare—and had to find my way back. That was when I began to discover the power of personal resiliency.

He came home that Sunday evening, later than I had expected him, but he was ready to spend the evening as we had planned. I had tried to reach him to tell him how sick I was feeling, but he hadn't answered any of my calls. Looking back on it, at first he seemed to take it in stride that we couldn't have the family evening we had planned; I didn't see what was coming. An hour or so later, as I still sat with my youngest child and his homework and my migraine pounded, I saw the storm of my husband's temper had begun.

I had long believed I had a personal relationship with God. Since my teenage years, I had embraced the concept of a universal, loving force I came to call God: Spirit, and Love, an eternal presence for All, an omnipresent force of Good in my life and the Universe. I often prayed, and asked for the strength to be the kind of wife, mother and daughter I wanted to be. I asked for guidance, for wisdom, for endurance, for peace. I asked for relief from daily strains, from money pressures and career disappointments. I held gratitude for my husband, three beautiful children and for all our health. I did my best, worked hard, and was devoted to my husband, children, and parents.

I tried to live by the Golden Rule—Do unto others, as you would have them do unto you. Often it seemed my prayers went unnoticed, but my faith stayed constant. I believed, more than anything, that Love could conquer all.

I went to our bedroom to try to calm him. What happened next is very painful to remember. My husband of nearly 13 years, whom I had totally devoted my love and support to, lunged at me from behind the door. As my nine-year-old child watched from a few feet away, I was grabbed by the throat, pushed across our large bedroom into the bathroom, and choked. I remember starting to scream—and scream and scream. This time, I didn't stop screaming. I couldn't protect him —my husband—any more. This time I couldn't stop screaming.

I have often asked myself, "What made that time different? Why didn't I stop screaming that time, as I had in the past? What made it finally be enough? What gave me the strength to want to live? Why did I still even care?" There is only one answer I find no matter how many times I ask the question: Spirit.

Spirit within me. The presence of Love, keeping me alive, giving me the presence of mind not to give up, not to give in. The Flame that lives within us all, keeping me alive, in spite of years of physical, emotional and psychological abuse. Spirit prevailed and wouldn't let me give in. My prayers had, in fact, been heard.

My daughter, 11 years old at the time, heard me screaming and called the police. "My dad is trying to kill my mom," she told 911, "and I think he's going to come after me and my brother next!"

I finally left him. I took my terrified, traumatized children and left that life, that town, that world. Numb with shock and grief and pain and disbelief, we left it all behind to start again. A dazed mother with her two young children, not able to comprehend the nightmare. My oldest child was 2000 miles away at college, trying to grasp what had happened.

But we did go on. One day at a time, one step at a time. I prayed every step of the way for the strength to take the next step. I didn't even know what to pray for any more—or who or what I was praying to. But I felt some untold presence holding that little bit of flame still alive within me, giving me the strength to get up every day, feed the kids, and help them get through another day. Through the endless court dates, the criminal trial against him, and then the hideous, vindictive divorce. Tears I thought would never stop. Questions from my children I didn't know how to answer. Answers I thought would never come. One day at a time, one breath at a time, one step at a time.

I didn't realize how deeply my trust had been broken. I never knew how pervasive the effects of this trauma were on every aspect of my life. Perhaps the deepest, most elusive effect was that I didn't trust myself.

Most of us live with too much stress in our lives. Money problems, family problems, pressures from work, kids, spouses, partners, health. Over time, we can begin to lose sight of Trust. Many of us respond to pressure by trying harder to control everything and everyone around us. We try harder to change our spouse or partner so they will make us happier. We try harder to make our kids "successful"—even to be someone they may not be. We try to look like models, pulled together at all times, calm, cool, collected, beautiful and successful. Always striving for more, we work harder and harder to control every action of everyone around us in order to accomplish the outcome we think is best.

What we fail to notice along the way is the harder we try to control everything, the less things go our way. We get into more fights with the people we love. We get into more power struggles with our co-workers, our bosses, and our families. We begin to realize nothing is easy any more—it all feels like hard work! This is when I realized I didn't trust anyone or anything.

Letting go of my desperate attempts to control my world has allowed me to breathe a little more deeply, and peacefully. Most importantly I've begun to realize that what is right for me isn't necessarily right for someone else. The world doesn't stop turning on its axis just because the outcome isn't what I expected. Trying this, one incident at a time, has helped to rebuild my Trust.

Time has passed, and it is still sometimes hard to believe it all happened. Through all this, the flame inside of me that was literally almost extinguished has slowly begun to burn brighter and stronger. The well of my Self, that had dried up to almost nothingness, is being replenished. The tears I have shed, and sometimes still do, wash out depths of grief, sorrow and pain for broken dreams, shattered promises, fantasies never realized, love lost. In their place have risen new dreams, new hope, new horizons lit with the first blush of morning and the last glow of the moon and stars. The journey has taken me through the dark, tar-thick river of a nightmare to reach the other side. The journey taught me enormous personal resiliency.

There have been a few specific tools I embraced along the way that have helped me to rebuild my life, one moment at a time. These are:

- Personal Prayer (I don't actually attend a church)
- Journaling
- Affirmations (I even post them around my house!)
- Reading spiritual books
- Writing poetry
- Exercise
- Being out in nature
- Friends
- Turning the pain, confusion and frustration over to my Higher Power.

Each one of these tools has become a regular, vital, and stabilizing force in my life. They serve as consistent reminders, refresh me, reinforce my courage, and help me in the moment to reconnect with my evolving spirit and strength, with my Higher Power.

I went back to college almost two years ago, to finally continue the education and career preparation I had begun more than 25 years ago. I decided to speak out about my experience and now travel nationally and internationally to speak on domestic violence. I am close to the completion of my graduate program to become a psychotherapist. I will pursue my doctorate degree as I work in my field.

I have to work every day to learn to Trust again, to welcome my Spirit, to embrace that Higher Power and universal force of Goodness that dwells within us all. I had to learn to find it, and hear it, and Trust it, after coming so close to losing it forever. I had it all within me, all the time. You do, too.

Having emerged from a critical life situation, KATHRYN TULL has transformed her life and shares her inspiring message around the country as a speaker and trainer. A single mother of three and long-time non-profit management specialist, Kathryn is completing her graduate degree in clinical and community psychology. She is a nationally certified trainer for Adults and Children Together Against Violence (ACT). She can be reached directly at 310.920.9480 or visit online at www.nextboldstep.com.

ABOUT THE AUTHORS

The women who contributed to this book come from diverse backgrounds and have mastered a wide range of skills and approaches. They are TV executives, financial asset managers, relationship coaches, personal organizers, educators, psychotherapists, hypnotherapists, account executives, and more. Many have worked for enterprises ranging from Fortune 500 companies to small businesses, though most are now entrepreneurs. The one thing that unites them is success. Every one of them has demonstrated effectiveness and excellence in their endeavors. How can we know this? Results. Though not names you might recognize instantly, many of these women have been featured on national television and in national magazines. All have something to say worth knowing. Together they have contributed to a book that is greater than the sum of its parts.

FRONT ROW: Stephanie Frank, Wendy Robbins, Alice Aspen March, Kathleen Mierswa, Meri Anne Beck-Woods, Natalie Pace, Madeleine LaFontaine, Jeanne Peters, MaryLou Kenworthy, Julie Ferman

SECOND ROW: Lillian Bajor, Kathryn Tull, Rachel Hart, Deborah Koppel-Mitchell, Andrea Butler, Kim Castle, Elisa Goodman, Morgana Rae, Beth Schneider, Audrey Reed, Dee Behrman, Christine Kloser, Jentana Dabbs, Yvonne Thomas, Julie Hayes, JJ Flizanes

THIRD ROW: Veronica Crystal Young, Lisa Haisha, Melissa Rose, Mabel Katz, Lisa Cherney, Arvee Robinson, Shawn Moore, Heather Rem, Victoria Kindle Hodson, Adelaide Smith,

BACK ROW: Cindi Pringle, Debbie Friedman, Barbara Schiffman, Mariaemma Pelullo-Willis, Ann Convery

Find out more about the authors at:
www.InspirationToRealization.com

ABOUT CHRISTINE KLOSER

Christine Kloser, Author, Television Host, and Founder of the Network for Empowering Women Entrepreneurs (NEW) is an entrepreneur extraordinaire. Christine has coached, advised and inspired thousands of women to take charge of their personal, financial, spiritual and business lives. She is a pioneer in bridging the gap between business and spirituality.

Christine has been a guest on numerous local/national radio and TV shows. Her insightful articles and quotes have appeared in a variety of publications from coast to coast including the books, *What Nobody Ever Tells You About Starting Your Own Business* and *Visionary Women Inspiring The World*. A proud member of the Who's Who of Empowering Executives and Professionals, Christine was also recognized for winning the 2004 Wealthy Woman "Business Ambassador" Award for her dedication to empowering women entrepreneurs.

This book extends the benefits of her creativity and experience to women around the world. Christine is headquartered in Los Angeles, and is available for coaching, lectures and seminars.

To learn more about Christine Kloser, please contact her at:

Christine Kloser
c/o NEW Entrepreneurs, Inc.
PO Box 661274
Los Angeles, CA 90066
Ph: (310) 745-0794
Fax: (310) 745-0841
Email: christine@christinekloser.com
Web: www.christinekloser.com.

WHAT'S YOUR STORY?

If sharing our experiences has assisted you to new levels of success in your life and/or business, we would love to hear from you. We expect to be publishing more volumes like this in the future, and perhaps your story would assist other women to follow their hearts and souls. We also publish inspiring stories on our website, www.NEWentrepreneurs.com.

You needn't be concerned with how polished your story is. Just get us the idea in 1500 words. If necessary we'll help with the editing to whip it into shape. The main thing is that we share our successes so that all of us can know that anyone who wants to—not just those who have already done it—can have the life they choose.

Naturally, we would contact you if we were considering putting your story into publication.

Email your material to us at info@newentrepreneurs.com. In the subject line please write: Inspiration Story Submission.

We look forward to hearing from you.

> Sincerely,
> Christine Kloser

COULD YOU USE SOME WEEKLY INSPIRATION AND TOOLS TO HELP YOU TURN YOUR DREAMS INTO REALITY?

Subscribe to "The Empowered Woman" Ezine

The Empowered Woman Ezine is published weekly by NEW Entrepreneurs, Inc. It is designed for women who want weekly success tips, articles, resources, motivation and tools to help them turn their "Inspiration to Realization!"

This FREE ezine provides you with opportunities to:

- Connect with other like-minded women
- Be invited to FREE tele-seminars that help you achieve personal, business, financial and spiritual fulfillment
- Discover resources to save you time and money
- Enjoy educational and motivational articles
- And much more!

Subscribe now to receive weekly editions of *The Empowered Woman Ezine* and you receive a FREE special report, *The Top 3 Challenges for Women Entrepreneurs and How YOU Can Avoid Them.*

To learn more and sign up now, please visit:
www.NEWnewsletter.com

Network for Empowering Women
Helping Women Ignite Their Business And Fuel Their Soul™

JOIN THE NETWORK FOR EMPOWERING WOMEN (NEW)!

BE PART OF AN ORGANIZATION THAT IS DEDICATED TO YOUR PERSONAL, BUSINESS, FINANCIAL AND SPIRITUAL FULFILLMENT!

You're invited to join the Network for Empowering Women (NEW)

It is the only professional women's association that combines business and financial development with personal and spiritual fulfillment.

WHY JOIN NEW? Women join for many reasons including: professional development, networking, visibility, inspiration, motivation, education, friendship, personal fulfillment and camaraderie. (Not to mention the $7,000+ member benefit package.)

WHO JOINS NEW? Every woman in this book is a member of NEW. They are a solid representation of the caliber, diversity and like-mindedness of the members of NEW. Some members have been in business over 25 years and others are just getting started. There is something for everyone.

WHERE DO MEMBERS LIVE? Members can live anywhere. In addition to our in-person meetings and seminars, we also offer monthly virtual meetings and tele-classes so women everywhere can network with each other and learn tools and skills to help them succeed... in all areas of life.

HERE ARE A FEW OF THE NEW MEMBER BENEFITS YOU'LL RECEIVE:

✔ FREE "Breakthrough to Success" seminar with Christopher Howard

✔ FREE 3-Day "Millionaire Mind Intensive" training with T. Harv Eker. PLUS, you can bring a guest for FREE!

✔ FREE Enlightened Millionaire Retreat with Mark Victor Hansen and Robert Allen, Co-authors of *One Minute Millionaire*

✔ FREE member directory listing and web page in the NEW online directory

✔ FREE access to our online Success Audio Library

✔ FREE e-zine advertisements in "The Empowered Woman" weekly newsletter

✔ FREE teleclasses and virtual meetings.

✔ $250 DISCOUNT "BrandU Workshop"

✔ DISCOUNTS to all NEW events

✔ FREE 45-minute web site consultation

✔ And a lot more!

What is the annual membership fee? Only $197.

Start your benefits now at:
www.NEWentrepreneurs.com

ALSO BY LOVE YOUR LIFE:

Stepping Up to the Plate
Inspiring Interviews with Major Leaguers
by David Kloser

Love Your Life books may be purchased
for educational, business or sales
promotion use.

For information please write:
Special Markets Department,
Love Your Live
PO Box 661274
Los Angeles, CA 90066

or email
booksales@loveyourlife.com